School Finance Elections

A Comprehensive Planning Model for Success

Don E. Lifto and J. Bradford Senden

Published in partnership with the
American Association of School Administrators

ScarecrowEducation
Lanham, Maryland • Toronto • Oxford
2004

Published in partnership with
the American Association of School Administrators

Published in the United States of America
by ScarecrowEducation
An imprint of The Rowman & Littlefield Publishing Group, Inc.
4501 Forbes Boulevard, Suite 200, Lanham, Maryland 20706
www.scarecroweducation.com

PO Box 317
Oxford
OX2 9RU, UK

Copyright © 2004 by Don E. Lifto and J. Bradford Senden

All rights reserved. No part of this publication may be reproduced, stored in a retrieval system, or transmitted in any form or by any means, electronic, mechanical, photocopying, recording, or otherwise, without the prior permission of the publisher.

British Library Cataloguing in Publication Information Available

Library of Congress Cataloging-in-Publication Data

Lifto, Don E., 1949–
 School finance elections : a comprehensive planning model for success / Don E. Lifto ; J. Bradford Senden.
   p. cm.
 "Published in partnership with the American Association of School Administrators."
 Includes bibliographical references and index.
 ISBN 1-57886-111-X (pbk. : alk. paper)
 1. Education—United States—Finance. 2. School elections—United States—Planning. 3. School taxes—United States. I. Senden, J. Bradford, 1949– II. American Association of School Administrators. III. Title.
LB2825 .L485 2004
371.2'06—dc22
                                                        2003024112

∞™ The paper used in this publication meets the minimum requirements of American National Standard for Information Sciences—Permanence of Paper for Printed Library Materials, ANSI/NISO Z39.48-1992.
Manufactured in the United States of America.

Contents

List of Figures, Tables, and Maps	v
Foreword	vii
Acknowledgments	ix
Introduction	xi
1 Research to Practice	1
2 The Voter File and Count Book	9
3 Looking Back to Plan Forward	17
4 Mapping	25
5 Community Survey	45
6 Ballot Questions	63
7 Ongoing and Targeted Communications	69
8 Planning	83
9 Leadership and Organization	97
10 Execution of Campaign	105
A Final Thought	123
Bibliography	125
Index	129
About the Authors	131

Figures, Tables, and Maps

FIGURES

I.1	Comprehensive Planning Model	xii
5.1	The Uninformed Benchmark	52
5.2	The Informed Benchmark	56
5.3	A Parent Cross-Tabulation	57
6.1	Use of Ballot-Splitting to Alter Voting Patterns	66
7.1	Targeted Flier Examples	76
7.2	Targeted Flier Examples	77
7.3	Targeted Flier Examples	78
7.4	Turtle Theme	82
10.1	Campaign Organization	106
10.2	Targeting Voters	117

TABLES

4.1	Precinct-by-Precinct Results	26
4.2	District Precinct Characteristics	38
5.1	Community Survey Questions	53

MAPS

4.1	"Yes" Percentage	28
4.2	Percentage of Registered Parents	29
4.3	Percentage Democratic	31
4.4	Percentage of Very Active Voters	32
4.5	Median Age	34
4.6	Median Household Income	35
4.7	Median Assessed Value	37
4.8	Polling Place	40
4.9	Voter Contact	41
4.10	Door-to-Door	42
4.11	Single City Block	43

Foreword

The role of school system leader has broadened and become more complex over the last few decades. There was a time when leaders could be effective by being "B" keepers—overseeing buildings, buses, books, budgets, and bonds. Now the task has broadened so that leaders must also be master of the "Cs" of education—communication, collaboration, community building, and child advocacy. In this book, Don Lifto and Brad Senden have found a way to wed these two obligations.

School leaders must find a way to provide places for learning that are appropriate to the task and, through their symbolism, tell children that they are valued *and* that learning is important. This calls for finding ways to renovate outmoded and deteriorating structures and for providing new spaces for a new generation of children. That takes money. And that money must come from the community through its willingness to tax itself for that purpose.

The passage of tax and bond levies was probably never easy, but in today's climate where personal greed is seen as good and the public is told repeatedly that "it is not the government's money; it is your money" this is a tough sell. The challenge is even greater since only about 25% of the population has school-age children and, therefore, is directly concerned with what happens in schools. School leaders must not only be adept at planning for school needs, they also have to be political salespersons who can sell the public on the schools' needs and convince them they need to put aside their private needs for the public good.

But merely doing a great sales job is not enough. The public is inundated with messages from marketers selling everything from libations to lifestyle. People are saturated and more than a little wary. Although school leaders need to understand the tools of marketing, they need to go beyond that to be adept at ongoing engagement with the public. School finance elections are not won through a campaign—they are won through the development of an ongoing relationship with the public. That calls for leaders who know how to effectively engage the public throughout the year.

School leaders also need to be able to call upon the new tools available for doing the job. They need to be able to research the best ways to plan their approach to the public and to use the technological tools available to carry out these approaches. This book provides an overview of all this, and more.

Leadership is about more than planning for budgets or bonds. It is about understanding the human heart and using that understanding to create a connection between the heart and the head. This allows a leader to move people to do what they know they need to do to make a better community. Lifto and Senden have provided a primer on bridging the Bs and the Cs of leadership and using the bridge as a way of connecting the schools to their community.

Paul D. Houston
Executive Director
American Association of School Administrators

Acknowledgments

For the two of us, writing this book has been a labor of love and an opportunity to put to paper what we have learned about school finance elections over more than two decades. Some of the learning has been research-based and theoretical in nature, and for that knowledge we thank our teachers—the professors, researchers, political pundits, and various experts who have shared their wisdom over the years. Much of the learning was on-the-job training, honing our skills in the trenches of dozens of election wars, working hand-in-hand with superintendents, school board members, principals, parent leaders, and countless campaign volunteers. Although the thrill of victory is certainly more fun, we have learned just as much from the tears of unfulfilled expectations. For these experiences and the opportunity to work with hundreds of talented people we are grateful.

We also want to thank and acknowledge our able editor, Carrie Smith, for her assistance with copyediting.

Lastly, and most importantly, we thank our families for their love and support throughout our careers and, in particular, for their encouragement to complete what we hope will be an important book for school administrators and school districts as they strive to meet the facility and financial needs of public school students at the ballot box.

Introduction

"Education officials need to furnish leadership in school elections. . . . An unsuccessful election reduces educational opportunities for students" (Kimbrough & Nunnery, 1971, p. 4). Who can argue with this simple statement? Providing effective leadership, however, is not that easy. Research and practice have yet to yield an election formula that always produces winners. Whether it is a request for bricks and mortar or more operating money, each election type and context are unique with no guarantee that a set of campaign strategies—successful in one district—will not fail in your community. If successful campaigns were *not* such a delicate balance of science and art, the key to success would have long since been discovered, resulting in significantly more school districts winning at the ballot box.

This book represents a marriage of research and successful practice, presenting a comprehensive planning model for school leaders preparing for and conducting school finance elections. Information presented emphasizes systems and strategies rather than specific campaign tactics. Avoiding a myopic focus on tactics allows school leaders to elevate their thinking to a more comprehensive and long-range vision of election planning. Each of the chapters elaborates on one of the 10 elements in our comprehensive planning model (see Figure I.1). Use of this model has reaped success in all types of school districts from New Jersey to California, and we hope that it brings you success at the ballot box as well.

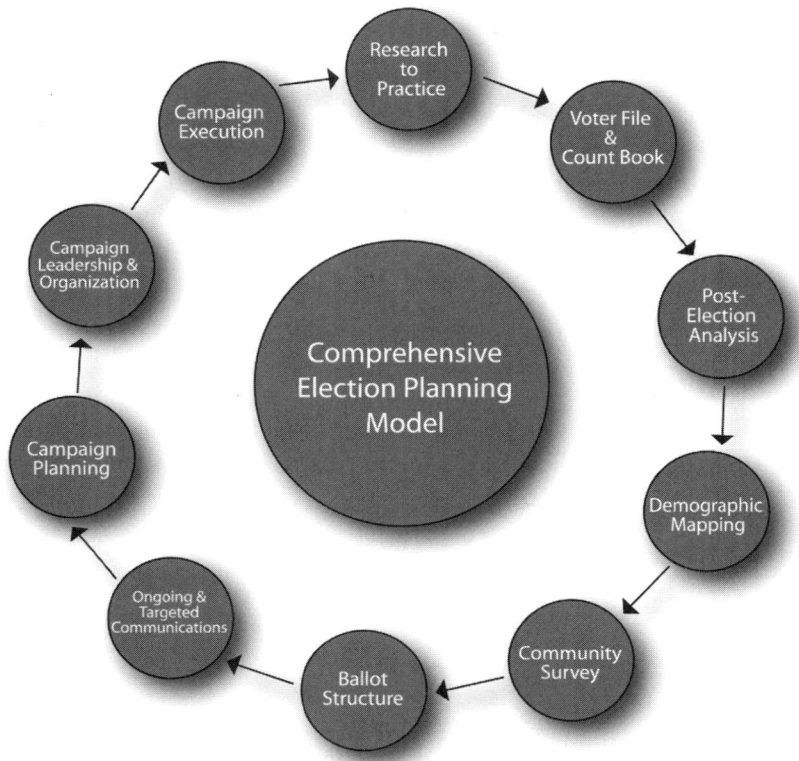

Figure I.1. Comprehensive Planning Model

ELEMENT 1: RESEARCH TO PRACTICE

Although there is no pat formula for success, school leaders should not be discouraged from rolling up their sleeves, digging in, and becoming students of sound research and successful practices. In the final analysis, there is no better road map to a successful election. In fact, university libraries are replete with dissertations documenting that winning campaigns use research-based strategies to a *greater extent* and *more effectively* than unsuccessful elections. Understanding the research on school finance elections and thoughtfully implementing these strategies are the foundations of winning campaigns.

ELEMENT 2: VOTER FILE AND COUNT BOOK

The voter file and count book represent the district's master election dossier detailing essential information about the key resource in your campaign—the voters. By integrating files of registered voters, parents, preschool families, and past supporters, the campaign the district is planning is provided with a powerful tool for planning, canvassing, targeting messages, and getting-out-the-vote strategies.

ELEMENT 3: POSTELECTION ANALYSIS

It is important to keep one eye on the rearview mirror as you drive toward your next election. A thorough understanding and analysis of prior elections in your district is a prerequisite to effectively executing your next campaign. By integrating data from voting records with the parent file, school leaders can gain a more precise understanding of past voter participation and, therefore, can better predict future voter behavior. We have coined the acronym CASA to describe this process (collect, analyze, summarize, and archive).

ELEMENT 4: DEMOGRAPHIC MAPPING

Demographic mapping merges current census data, containing a multitude of information about the district, with registered voter and parent data found in the annotated voter file. This information is displayed in color maps and provides school and volunteer leaders with a better understanding of the school district and strategic information from which to plan and execute the campaign.

ELEMENT 5: COMMUNITY SURVEY

Achieving alignment between the community's values and appetite for spending and what the school district actually needs and puts on the ballot is paramount to success. A random sample of registered voters is drawn from the annotated voter file, which mirrors the demography of the school district. The community survey, typically based on a 12- to

14-minute telephone interview administered three to six months prior to the election date, provides the school district with vital information about what the community thinks and what it is likely to support.

ELEMENT 6: BALLOT QUESTION

When the voters enter the voting booth, what will they see? In most states, ballots can contain a single proposal or multiple questions. Will each of the ballot questions be freestanding (i.e., winning or losing on their own merits) or will passage of the second or third question be contingent on the first proposal getting a thumbs up? The decision about the content and structure of the ballot is critical and must be guided by the district's election history and the results of the community survey.

ELEMENT 7: ONGOING AND TARGETED COMMUNICATIONS

Developing a compelling message and directing it to parents just prior to an election used to be good enough, but not anymore. In today's election environment, providing high-quality, ongoing communication throughout the year is essential. The election campaign builds on this foundation by developing core and subordinate messages and targeting them to unique audiences. The annotated voter file and cross-tabulated results found in the community survey provide the data from which to plan an effective communication strategy.

ELEMENT 8: TASKS AND TIMELINES

Planning and executing a school finance campaign is, for most school administrators, the most complex and challenging leadership task they will encounter. A common reason for failure is lack of coordination between what the school district is doing and the activities of volunteers working in support of the election. Remember, if there isn't a written plan, it does not exist. Key campaign activities must be spelled out, coordinated, and scheduled on a day-to-day and week-to-week basis to ensure that no one drops the ball.

ELEMENT 9: CAMPAIGN LEADERSHIP

Merely understanding the need to involve the community in a grassroots effort falls well short of the target when it comes to successful finance elections. Your campaign can be well on its way toward a victory if you are strategic and focused on recruiting the "ideal task performer" for each and every leadership need. Do not send your campaign volunteers out into the community until they are thoroughly prepared and trained.

ELEMENT 10: CAMPAIGN EXECUTION

Pick your analogy—sports, ballet, business, or politics—they're one in the same. All the research, planning, and training in the world will not matter if the school district, in cooperation with the campaign committee, cannot effectively execute the plan. The efforts of the school district and campaign committee must be driven by passion and an unrelenting commitment to be successful and girded by high-quality execution from beginning to end.

Now it's time to dive into the details. Each chapter builds upon the last as we provide school-system leaders with sound advice about the planning and execution of school finance elections.

CHAPTER 1

Research to Practice

You thought you did everything right. You devoured the research, interrogated winning superintendents from Albuquerque to Kalamazoo, and replicated successful campaign strategies from neighboring school districts. But when the ballots were finally counted, you found yourself on the losing end of an important school finance election. What happened?

Since there is no pat formula for success, school leaders should roll up their sleeves, dig in, and become students of sound research and successful practices. In the final analysis, there is no better road map to a successful election. In fact, university libraries are replete with dissertations documenting that winning campaigns use research-based strategies to a *greater extent* and *more effectively* than unsuccessful ones. Understanding the research on school finance elections and thoughtfully implementing these strategies form the foundation of a successful campaign.

To begin with, it is important to avoid a potentially shortsighted focus on campaign tactics and achieve a more comprehensive understanding of the research related to school finance elections. Without a basic understanding of the research-based variables most often associated with success, school leaders can easily slip into a frantic strategy of piecing together a hodgepodge of tactics from the archives of successful elections. Distributing the top 10 reasons to vote "yes" inside fortune cookies might have been a hit in a neighboring district, but this tactic could bomb in your community unless done within the context of a comprehensive, research-based election plan. School leaders need to understand that broad campaign strategies and the specific tactics to achieve them must be built upon and flow from a foundation of election research.

The research of Philip Piele and John Hall, completed 30 years ago, still provides the foundation for many contemporary dissertations and scholarly works on this topic. *Budgets, Bonds, and Ballots* (1973) summarizes more than a decade of research by analyzing and categorizing 61 election variables. Research studies for each of the variables are labeled as being significantly positive, negative, or not statistically related to the results of these elections. Their research summary emphasizes the difference between contextual variables (e.g., wealth) that are generally out of the practitioner's control and specific campaign strategies selected by a school leader. Understanding and applying election research within the unique context of a school community is part of the art of leadership within this framework. The campaign plan then becomes a carefully woven fabric of strategies designed to interact with and influence the environment within the school district. Dozens of other authors build on Piele and Hall's "megastudy," carrying the research forward into the present day. In the course of writing this book, we revisited the body of research conducted in the 1980s and 1990s but also analyzed more than 30 additional studies completed through 2002.

So, what have we learned about school elections over the last 30 years? In our experience, the following 11 factors are most often associated, in both research and practice, with successful school finance elections. In combination, they form the foundation for our planning model.

FACTOR 1: UNANIMOUS ELECTION RESOLUTION AND SUPPORT BY SCHOOL BOARD THROUGHOUT CAMPAIGN

School board solidarity is one of 20 variables examined by Piele and Hall (1973), with all studies pointing to a positive correlation between unanimity and successful elections. T. N. Pullium (1983) asserts that "total support by members of the school board is almost always necessary for the success of a school referendum" (p. 50). Another researcher more bluntly warns, "A school board whose members have not reached a consensus on the content and format of the referendum should not embark on a campaign" (Etheredge, 1989, p. 46). Blount (1991), Dunbar (1991), and Brummer (1999) cite similar findings. Clearly, this is a critical factor demanding attention long before a proposal is placed on the school board agenda.

FACTOR 2: COMMUNITY HAS HIGH LEVELS OF TRUST, SATISFACTION, AND PERCEPTIONS OF QUALITY FOR ITS PUBLIC SCHOOLS

School districts would be well advised to borrow from the Ford Motor Company tagline and make quality Job 1. Lifto and Morris (2000) focus on the quality question in their evaluation of 107 Minnesota school finance elections between 1996 and 2000. The common variable in each of the campaigns was pre-election polling, in which they asked, "How would you rate the quality of education in your public schools— excellent, good, only fair, or poor?"

How important is quality in relationship to school finance elections? In this study, 96% of the cases revealed that the size of the negative evaluation (i.e., fair or poor) discriminated between winning and losing campaigns. When more than 17% of the public gave their public schools fair or poor marks, 27 out of 30 elections failed. When less than 17% rated their schools as fair or poor, 76 out of 77 elections passed.[1] Maintaining a core value of quality as Job 1 is essential because "success at the polls is substantially driven by how your community views the quality of its public schools" (Lifto & Morris, 2000, p. 17). Studies by Corrick (1995), Phillips (1995), and Williamson (1997) echo the importance of residents' perceptions of quality and continuous improvement.

FACTOR 3: COMPREHENSIVE CAMPAIGN PLANNING AND EFFECTIVE EXECUTION BASED ON CURRENT RESEARCH, BEST PRACTICES, AND DEMOGRAPHIC CHARACTERISTICS OF THE COMMUNITY

The ability to understand and effectively apply election research in a particular context is critical and positively correlates with success.

More than three decades of research emphasize the importance of comprehensive planning and use of research-based strategies. Piele and Hall (1973), acting as pragmatists, remind school leaders that using research, conducting comprehensive planning, and then executing a world-class campaign are all within the control of the practitioner and *do* matter. J. F. Henderson Jr.'s study of Colorado school elections matches election outcomes with use of nine key campaign strategies. The more these factors were used, the more likely the election was successful (Henderson, 1986). Underscoring that a cookie-cutter approach does not work, Williamson (1997) concludes that school districts are more successful when research and campaign strategies are adapted to the community's values and demographic characteristics.

FACTOR 4: OUTSTANDING PUBLIC RELATIONS THROUGHOUT THE YEAR, TAILORED TO UNIQUE AUDIENCES WITHIN THE DISTRICT AND FOCUSED ON THE PURPOSE, BENEFITS, AND CONSEQUENCES OF A SUCCESSFUL OR UNSUCCESSFUL ELECTION

Serving as a foundation for successful finance elections, the quality of public engagement and related communication strategies are evident throughout the research. The most successful districts achieve three key attributes when it comes to public relations:

- Outstanding quality
- Ongoing public relations
- Focused messages to different audiences emphasizing the proposal's purpose and benefits

One researcher highlighted the need for ongoing engagement by warning campaigners not to "commit the fatal error [of] trying to educate the electorate while at the same time urging school supporters to vote" (Etheredge, 1989, p. 34). As the percentage of registered voters with children who are public school students continues to decrease, it is also important to develop the capacity to communicate multiple messages to a number of audiences. Several researchers, including Lode (1999) and Hinson (2001), would join the choir in emphasizing similar conclusions.

FACTOR 5: SCIENTIFIC POLLING IS USED TO BETTER UNDERSTAND THE COMMUNITY'S PERCEPTIONS, UNDERSTANDING, AND READINESS FOR PROPOSAL

Designing and administering a scientific poll drawn from the school district's registered voter file is one of the most important pre-election activities and positively correlates with success. In addition to testing the community's understanding and support for the district's proposal, surveys also provide the opportunity to benchmark key community perceptions (e.g., overall quality or financial management), some of which are linked with success and all of which will help target effective communications to key audiences. Basing decisions on reliable survey data is a potent political strategy closely tied to winning elections and integral to effective campaign communication. Dalton (1995) and Henderson (1997) each authored contemporary studies linking scientific surveys to success.

FACTOR 6: PROPOSAL REFLECTS STRONG ALIGNMENT BETWEEN ITS PURPOSE AND COST AND THE COMMUNITY'S PRIORITIES AND WILLINGNESS TO PAY HIGHER TAXES

School leaders must determine how to align the ballot question with what the community wants because "each district has its own collective demand for education under varying tax cost conditions" (Sclafani, 1985, p. 25). When it comes to school finance elections, alignment has two dimensions: the "what" or content of the proposal and the "how much" or the cost and tax impact. A campaign supporting the district has an advantage when the ballot question is congruent on both counts, aligning with the values of the community *and* its collective willingness to pay in the form of higher property taxes. Dalton (1995), Galton (1996), and Brummer (1999) document similar results.

FACTOR 7: BROAD-BASED AND STRATEGIC COMMUNITY INVOLVEMENT IN PLANNING AND EXECUTING A CAMPAIGN

Although "flying under the radar" may be an appealing approach in some communities, the preponderance of evidence suggests that broad, strategic community involvement is paramount to success in most circumstances. Few communities enjoy the luxury of having public school children in more than one-third of their households. As a result, if a district expects to garner sufficient support to pass the election, significant community involvement is usually the only option. It is important to note that community involvement has important quantitative *and* qualitative dimensions. Elections are more successful when the ideal task performers are recruited for specific campaign functions. Henderson (1997), Brummer (1999), and Lode (1999) are just a few of the many researchers who have positively correlated broad community involvement with successful elections.

FACTOR 8: EFFECTIVE USE OF VOTER FILE AND OTHER INTEGRATED DATABASES TO TARGET, CANVASS, AND DELIVER "YES" VOTERS TO THE POLLS

One of the challenges facing school leaders during a school finance election is to "remember that a referendum is a political—not an education—campaign" (Etheredge, 1989, p. 39). Grassroots committees seeking to elect candidates to local, state, and national office have long relied on registered voter files as the backbone of effective campaign work. It is the voter history files, parent files, and past-supporter archives that provide key data for voter targeting, focused communications, and get-out-the-vote efforts. Drawing the random sample for the survey from the voter history file allows the campaign to link key survey findings with particular blocs of citizens in the voter file and their likelihood of voting in the school finance election. Quantitative and qualitative studies by researchers such as True (1996), Williamson (1997), and Lode (1999) support the use of data to target, canvass, and effectively get the "yes" voters to the polls.

FACTOR 9: SUCCESS IN OBTAINING KEY VIP AND ORGANIZATIONAL ENDORSEMENTS

"The personal influence of influentials (opinion leaders) may be a critical factor in legitimizing (making acceptable) school proposals among voters" (Kimbrough & Nunnery, 1971, pp. 50–54). Identifying and engaging the power structure within a community can be a significant factor in determining an election's outcome. Doing so can be easier in smaller, more-stable communities as compared with sprawling suburbs where influence is more diffused. Endorsements from the media and key organizations can also be very helpful in building a base of community support. Developing relationships with these individuals and groups should be an important ongoing component of community engagement strategies. True (1996) and Stockton (1996) cite the positive influence of endorsements.

FACTOR 10: ABSENCE OF COMMUNITY CONFLICT AND AVOIDANCE OF ORGANIZED OPPOSITION

Significant community conflict and the organized opposition it often yields are difficult to overcome even with the best of campaigns. The distraction of conflict is bad enough, but even worse is that "citizens stimulated to vote by this community conflict have a tendency to cast negative ballots" (Chandler, 1989, pp. 21–22). Although it is impossible to control this variable completely, school leaders can use two strategies to minimize the damage. First, while "it may be impossible to eliminate tax resistance, . . . it can be controlled by attempting to reduce other controversies" (Allen, 1985, p. 94). For example, if your district needs to redo elementary boundaries, perhaps it can wait until after the election. School leaders should also attempt to "negotiate positions between influentials . . . so that the needs of education and children are not held hostage by two warring factions" (Kimbrough & Nunnery, 1971, pp. 22–23). Galton (1996), Day (1996), and Franklin (1997) authored other studies documenting the effect of conflict and organized opposition.

FACTOR 11: SUCCESSFUL BOND ELECTIONS OFTEN INCLUDE FUNDING FOR TECHNOLOGY AND INFORMATION ABOUT SITE-SPECIFIC IMPROVEMENTS

For the community that may be more self-centered and less egalitarian than in the past, communicating site-specific improvements is increasingly important. Many voters will be influenced by how the proposed improvements will affect *their* children or *their* neighborhood school. The almost universal desire for a school district to remain technologically advanced can also be a key factor. In a study of Oklahoma bond campaigns, Beckham (2001) found that elections were six times more likely to pass if they included an investment in technology. The higher the investment, the more likely the election would pass. Other researchers, including Williamson (1997) and Hockersmith (2001), drew parallel conclusions.

Research matters, regardless of whether it is quantitative studies and chi-square tests or qualitative studies and triangulation. Hundreds of studies have been done during the last 30 years against a backdrop of tens of thousands of school finance elections. This adds up to a substantial body of research and successful practice from which to draw. It is incumbent upon school leaders to build their election planning on this foundation and develop research-based strategies appropriate for their unique contexts. By doing so, more school districts will be successful on election day, and more students will have their educational needs met in our nation's public schools.

NOTE

1. The null hypothesis—that quality had nothing to do with elections success or failure—was rejected at the 0.005 level.

CHAPTER 2

The Voter File and Count Book

Like Biff in *Back to the Future II*, we have all had the fantasy that we can see the future and make a killing by either buying the right lottery ticket or betting on the right team. However, it is impossible to develop a clear view of the future by traveling through time. Fortunately, school finance campaigns have access to resources offering a clear picture of the future. The first of these tools—one that dramatically increases the value of all other campaign tools—is a fully annotated voter file.

Strategically, an annotated voter file allows campaign organizers to predict who will vote in any upcoming election by looking at who has participated in the majority of a community's recent elections. This knowledge enables a campaign to focus its volunteer hours and campaign dollars where they will have the greatest impact. Rather than starting with a list of everyone with a telephone number or all the parents within the district, a campaign can explode out of the starting gate with a list of those residents most likely to vote in a community election. Furthermore, instead of assuming that all parents will vote in the election, the campaign can, for example, develop a list of those parents who have trouble getting to the polls. The purpose of a voter file is to maintain focus not only on the voters who will always vote but also on the campaign's supporters who might forget to cast a ballot. A voter file makes all campaign-related efforts more efficient and more effective.

Now for the details. A voter file is a list of all of the school district's registered voters. In this electronic age, the information is available in various forms from a variety of sources. The county elections office or the office of the secretary of state in your state capitol should be your first stop. When you find a source for voter information on the state or county level, request instructions for ordering voter data and order an electronic copy of the data to avoid the daunting task of typing voter records into your computer.[1]

WHERE DO I FIND VOTER FILES?

One website that can be very useful in looking for voter files from government sources is www.statelocalgov.net/index.cfn. For example, users can find the secretary of state's website for each of the 50 states. For private voter file vendors, try www.vcsnet.com, blaemire.com/voterfiles.htm, or www.aristotle.com/lists.asp. Each will take you to a major list vendor's site.

Voter files can also be purchased from commercial vendors. These companies often offer two benefits over data you can obtain from a governmental source. First, private vendors generally provide their data in user-friendly data environments. For example, a vendor's software package may allow the user to easily produce the lists and labels needed for an effective campaign. Other vendors provide lists to which additional data enhancements (e.g., phone numbers) have been added. Second, most vendors provide data that are in a uniform structure in which voter history information is already integrated. However, prior to purchasing voter data from a commercial vendor, you should inquire about any restrictions the vendor has placed on the data. For example, a vendor may sell you data for use in *one* mailing or *one* set of phone canvass lists and you will be charged if you use the data a second time.

Determining the source of your campaign's voter data will depend largely on the computer expertise of your volunteers. Specifically, your campaign will need the expertise of a database programmer if you acquire data in an unfamiliar software format. Although you will not need someone capable of supporting data needs of a Fortune 500 company, you will need someone comfortable with the manipulation of data in programs such as Excel, FoxPro, dBase, or Access.

> **WHAT DO I DO WITH A VOTER FILE?**
>
> - Count the number of voters in the community to more effectively plan your campaign.
> - Produce lists and labels for mail and phone contact with very specific, targeted audiences.
> - Store the results of all voter contact completed by the campaign.

Conversely, if your campaign acquires data in a ready-to-use software package, you will not need someone with data manipulation experience. However, you need to consider other limitations. Campaign software is designed to complete prespecified tasks based on the understanding of the private data vendor. Far too often, campaigns believe software can do anything. Nothing could be further from the truth. Your software must be designed to support the type of campaign you plan to run. Like every strategy in your campaign toolbox, you must have the right tool for your campaign.

Once you have identified a source for voter information, you need to know what you are looking for and the kind of information you can expect to find. The core of a voter file is the full legal name and residential address of each voter in the district. In addition, voter files generally contain a record of each individual's voting activity, the voting district or precinct[2] assigned to the individual's address, a telephone number, the date on which the person registered to vote, and the individual's date of birth. There also may be information about his or her party affiliation, race, birthplace, and/or mailing address.[3]

When requesting an electronic copy of your district's voter records, request a *file layout*. A file layout provides the names of the data fields contained in the voter file. For example, some voter files store the voter's name in three data fields: first name, middle name, and last name. Others provide you with one data field that separates the last name of the voter from the first and middle names with a comma. The file layout will tell you not only how the data are stored in the voter file but also the number of characters you can expect to find in each data field. Without file layout information you may not be able to successfully figure out where one data field begins and another ends. More important, without a file layout, you may not be able to tell what you have and, therefore, may discard valuable voter information.

Each piece of information in the voter file can be very useful in planning a school finance campaign. Some of the most important pieces of information are:

- *Residential address.* This information has obvious value if you want to write or visit a voter. It is also important because the address can be used to link the voter file to an electronic list of all parents in the district or an assessor's file. The residential address is also essential to append U.S. Census information into the voter file.
- *Mailing address.* In most cases, a voter's mailing address is the same as his or her residential address. There are, however, voters who have requested that any information from the registrar be mailed to an alternate address. There are also communities where the post office will only deliver to P.O. box addresses. In these communities you will need to use the mailing address given for each voter. The street addresses you will find in the voter file are part of the 911 emergency services system but are not used by the postal service.
- *Voting activity.* The amount of information about an individual's level of voting activity varies from state to state and from private vendor to private vendor. In some states (e.g., Minnesota, Indiana, and Kentucky), complete multiyear voter histories come with the voter file. In others (e.g., California) you will be asked to specify the election information you want. Unfortunately, some states (e.g., Wisconsin) are ill equipped, unprepared, or unwilling to provide such detailed information. Whatever the case, you want as much voter history as you can obtain, as a voter's individual record of voting activity provides a wealth of information about who will show up for your election.
- *Voting district or precinct.* Every address in a voter file is assigned to a voting district or precinct. This information is important for two reasons. First, you will want to generate lists sorted by precinct to facilitate the coordination of volunteer activities. Second, just prior to the election you can link a voter's precinct name to the polling place assigned to that precinct. Linking this information enables the campaign to tell voters where they will vote. Furthermore, knowing the precincts

is essential if you are campaigning in a state that allows poll watching and you intend to monitor polls on election day to see if your supporters are voting.
- *Registration date.* Knowing when a voter first registered provides a campaign with two valuable pieces of information. First, the registration date can be used as a proxy for the length of time a person has lived in the district. For example, if long-term community residents need a great deal of information about the school finance election, registration date information can help target them for supplemental communications. Second, the registration date can be used in conjunction with an individual's voting history to identify "future frequent voters." Voting history can be a powerful indicator of future voting activity.
- *Birth date.* An individual's birth date enables you to calculate an individual's age. If you find there are voters for whom there is no record of a birth date, do not panic. Simply find out if your elections office has always been required to ask for a birth date when individuals register to vote. If, for example, they have only been collecting birth dates for the last 10 or 15 years, your "no agers" are relatively long-term district residents. If there are no birth dates in the voter file, it is safe to assume that your state or county is probably still not collecting them.
- *Party affiliation.* Party-related data may come in a number of forms or may not be available at all. Some states (e.g., California and Kentucky) ask individuals to declare a party when they register. This generally means that everyone in the file will have either a party affiliation or record of his or her declaration to decline party selection. You may also find members of rather obscure parties—such as California's Middle Class Party, Rock & Roll Party, or Birthday Party—in your voter file. In other states (e.g., Indiana and Illinois), individuals select a party ballot when they opt to vote in the primary. This allows you to create a party affiliation by looking at the individual's primary voting history. Finally, some states (e.g., Minnesota) provide no meaningful party information.

School finance campaigns often begin with two assumptions. First, everyone supports the local schools. Second, parents are registered and will vote in the district's school finance election. Both are false. School elections fail nationwide because there are people who will vote "no" to a proposal. Not only are parents not always registered to vote but, even if they are registered, they easily forget to vote in school finance elections. Therefore, the basic voter file should include additional data (e.g., registered voters with school-age children) for targeted campaign-related communications efforts.

Furthermore, identifying registered parents enables the district to understand the parents' role in determining the school finance election's outcome. Armed with voting history data, the district can also determine how many of the registered parents have strong, vigorous voting records. This information is developed by comparing the names and addresses of the parents in the district with the names and addresses of the community's registered voters.

Equally valuable information includes voters in households with a recent district graduate, a donor to a school district education foundation or PTA, and parents of preschool-age children. If a district has been on the ballot previously, it is extremely important that its "past supporters" be identified in the current election's voter file. Unfortunately, far too often, such information is not preserved. The lists necessary to identify all these groups may not be available when the voter file is being prepared. If this is the case, some of this information can be purchased commercially and merged with the voter file information.

Beyond identifying specific individuals in the voter file, U.S. Census data can be used to enhance the file. Valuable information (e.g., median household age, median household income, ethnic and racial background, median home value, and educational attainment) can bolster a campaign's database. To link these data to the voter file, the file must be "geocoded," which means assigning a census tract or block group number to every address (or as many as technology will allow). Once you know the block group for a specific address, you can link the voter file at the block group level to census data. Such a link will not tell you definitively that an individual is in a specific income bracket or of a specific ethic group. It could tell you, however, whether you are dealing with a voter in a high-income or low-income neighborhood.

Finally, linking the voter file to the records of property value that are generally available from the county assessor allows you to separate properties with high and low assessed values as well as to more accurately identify rental properties. Assessor's data can be expensive but there are times (especially during a bond election during which the cost to each voter is based on their home's assessed value) when it is worth it.

"Counting" is the end product of the voter file preparation process. Once you have annotated the file as completely as possible, you will want to produce a *count book*. A count book quantifies all of the demographic features in the file. It provides the district and the campaign with a quick reference tool designed to better understand how many voters are, for example, male, parents, older than 65, or younger than 34.

Count books are generally organized so that the first page or "top sheet" presents counts for the file's important demographic features. Each subsequent page provides a similar complete demographic count for each individual demographic feature. Therefore, if the top sheet's

---

HOW DO I USE A COUNT BOOK?

Assume for a moment that we are in a school district that was able to build a voter file in which it identified current district parents, preschool parents, and the households from which students recently graduated.

The count book tells members of the campaign that there are 2,450 current parents living in 1,225 households. The voter file has phone numbers for 93% of these households. In addition, there are 1,004 preschool parents living in 502 households and 1,234 voters living in 616 households in which a student graduated from high school during the past five years. In both of these groups, the file has phone numbers for 90% of the households.

All these numbers allow the campaign to effectively plan for direct mail to these groups followed by a phone canvass. First, add all the households in all three groups. A mailing to parents, preschool parents, and the parents of recent graduates will involve 2,343 pieces of mail. If the campaign assumes that it will spend 75¢ per piece to print and mail the material it wants to provide to this audience, it now knows that it will cost $1,757.25 to execute this step in its campaign plan.

Next, the campaign can plan its phone canvass. Based on data in the count book, there are approximately 2,100 phone numbers available for this audience. If the campaign assumes a volunteer can complete 15 canvass calls per hour and each volunteer will call for two hours a night, it knows that it will take 10 volunteers seven nights to call all 2,100 of these households.

first two lines tell you how many voters are male and how many are female, the second page will provide a complete demographic picture of the district's male voters while the third page will provide the same data for the district's female voters. All data in the count book are essential to the campaign's planning and execution process and integral to the key strategies of voter identification, canvassing, targeted communications, and get-out-the vote efforts.

NOTES

1. The process of ordering data from state or county offices varies from state to state and often from county to county. More and more, all of the information needed will be available on a website. In many cases, however, someone will need to visit an elections office, fill out the paper work requesting voter data, and pick the data up when they are ready.

2. The voting district or precinct may also be called a ward, a beat, or a box.

3. You cannot see how an individual voted, but you can tell when they voted.

CHAPTER 3

Looking Back to Plan Forward

In describing its primetime hit *Crossing Jordan*, NBC's website touts star Jill Hennessy as "a sexy, smart and fearless Boston medical examiner with a penchant for going beyond the call of duty to investigate crimes." A growing fan base of forensic groupies tunes in weekly to watch Jordan "channel her inner anger towards piecing together complex murder cases that have been hidden, shoved aside—or conveniently forgotten." The clues, of course, must first be coaxed from the dead and then reassembled to understand what actually happened.

Albeit not sexy, school leaders must also be smart and fearless as they conduct the forensic studies needed to prepare for their next election. In this context, school leaders work on an examination table where the results of elections past await exploration. The fully annotated voter file contains the clues and secrets they seek. Similar to *Crossing Jordan*, this step has an investigative orientation and requires school leaders to discover and effectively use what is often "hidden, shoved aside—or conveniently forgotten."

ELECTION DAY IN YOUR REARVIEW MIRROR

Most school districts squander a key strategic opportunity when they fail to collect, analyze, summarize, and archive valuable data after every school finance election—an activity equally important following both successful and unsuccessful campaigns. The most obvious data analysis is to understand exactly who participated in the district's most recent school finance election. There are basic questions to be explored and answered. How did the campaign effort in support of the ballot question influence the electorate? How did various demographic groups (e.g., Very Active Voters, young males, and residents of the west side) vote relative to their proportionate share of the voter file? What does the long-term voting history of the individuals who cast ballots tell campaign planners about this election? These and many other questions can be probed in a postelection analysis, yielding critical information for school leaders planning an election campaign.

LESSONS FROM THE PAST

There are basic questions that need to be asked during a postelection analysis. The answers form the lesson from the past available to the planners of the district's next election.

- What type of election just occurred?
- When might this type of election occur again?
- Did parents participate in this school finance election?
- If parent participation was not uniform, are there parent groups that will need a little extra attention during the next election?
- Did identified nonparent supporters participate?
- What lessons are there in the participation of the nonparent supporters for those who must target the next campaign?
- Are there areas of the district that present unique challenges to the next campaign? The characteristics of these areas and the attitudes of the voters who live in them should be explored with maps and surveys.

The idea that a district should look back at its last election when planning the next one is based on the simple concept that the best predictors of future behavior are actions taken in the past. In this context, an understanding of who will vote in the next election begins with an understanding of who has voted in the district before.

A postelection analysis begins with the isolation of all the information available in the voter file about the population that voted in the district's most recent election. Once this population is isolated, all of its demographic characteristics are counted and compared with the population of all voters in the district. Specifically, the campaign needs to understand which demographic groups are over- or underrepresented in this population.

For example, the counts developed to identify the number of male and female voters that cast ballots is used to calculate the percentage of the total number of voters who participated who are male versus female. These percentages are then compared with the percentage of the entire voter file that is male or female. This process is repeated for each significant demographic feature. A typical result might show that although women make up 52% of all voters in the district, postelection research finds that women made up 56% of the population that voted. The district now knows that its last election attracted more women than men.

Knowing the election attracted more women allows the campaign to ask additional questions. Were these older or younger women? Since the parents were marked in the voter file, the campaign can determine how many of these women are the parents of school-age children. In addition, the campaign can find out if these are women with a long-term history of voting in every local election or women who generally do not vote. Each detail is a clue that allows campaign officials to create a picture of what happened on election day. That picture serves as a road map for the district's next school finance election.

What about the men in the district? If men are underrepresented in the population that voted, all the same questions are asked to determine the characteristics of male voters who missed this election. In one specific case, a postelection analysis found that a large number of the men who stayed home were younger parents with relatively weak voting histories. While their wives had gotten to the polls to vote for the school finance proposal, these potential parent "yes" votes failed to cast a ballot. As a result, the district added a male mentor program to its next campaign plan. A team of older male parents with good long-term voting records worked throughout the campaign to communicate directly with younger dads. At each step they emphasized the need not only to support the school district's proposal as a volunteer but also to vote "yes" on election day. They systematically communicated the importance of every vote. An analysis of the campaign results confirmed that it worked. Not only did turnout among younger male parents increase significantly but the district also turned a heartbreaking loss into a solid win.

Once the general nature of the voting population has been developed, a postelection analysis turns to look in detail at the performance among parents and the individual voters identified by the campaign as supporters of the district's school finance proposal.[1] Each group needs to be examined in two ways:

- How was each group represented on election day?
- Did almost all of the people in each group cast a ballot?

In both groups, overrepresentation is extremely important. For example, if parents represent 23% of the registered voter population, they are overrepresented if they constituted 36% of the population that voted on election day. In all cases, the campaign wants to find parents overrepresented in a school finance election. This is the result of two factors that exist in almost every school finance election. First, parents should be naturally attracted to a school finance election. Second, every school finance campaign must have a program designed to maximize the parent vote. Therefore, if parents are underrepresented in the population that voted on election day, something is very wrong. Either there was a serious flaw in the planning or execution of the campaign or the district's proposal was seriously out of alignment with the priorities of the parent population. Any district that finds itself in this situation has some major work ahead—work that must be completed before considering another school finance election.

Even when parents are overrepresented in the population that voted, the district needs to look at the degree to which the potential vote within the parent population was "maximized." For example, if parents represent 23% of the voter file but constitute 36% of the population that voted, an initial conclusion could be that parent participation in the election was strong. But, if only 43% of all registered parents took the time to cast a ballot, this initial conclusion would be wrong. Leaving 57% of the parent population at home on election day means the campaign supporting the district's finance proposal failed to maximize the parent vote. Such a situation can easily make the difference between an election day win and loss.

Knowing that parent participation might be a problem allows the district's next effort to structure its campaign plan to address this challenge. Where absentee voting is easy, campaigns very often plan to make sure all supportive parents with weak voting histories "vote by mail" long before election day. Such campaigns may even include an absentee ballot application so the recipient needs only to sign the form and wait for their ballot to arrive in the mail. Other campaigns have developed extensive "buddy systems." Similar to the older male mentor program, parents who can be counted on to vote are assigned a number of election buddies—that is, parents without solid voting records. Throughout the campaign, these parents systematically contact their "buddies" to emphasize the importance of every vote.

USING A POSTMORTEM TO TARGET

The results of a postelection analysis often cause a district to modify the way in which voters are targeted in the next campaign. For example, a large school district placed a bond proposal on the ballot and then executed an extremely weak communications effort in support of the proposal. As a result, the bond proposal failed to win voter support. In a postelection analysis, it became very clear that only one-third of the parent population had voted in this election.

In the second effort, parents were divided into two target groups. Group 1 was made up of those parents who, despite a weak communications effort, found out that a bond was on the ballot and voted. Group 2 comprised those parents who did not vote in the first election. Instead of incurring the cost of increasing the amount of mail and telephone contact made with all parents, the second campaign was able to focus an increased amount of contact where it was needed most—on the parents in Group 2. This group of parents received two to three times as much mail as the first group and was the focus of more telephone contact by campaign volunteers. The result was a large increase in parent participation and a win on election day.

A postelection analysis also involves a careful look at the nonparent voters identified by the campaign as supporting the district's finance proposal. Though many techniques can be used to identify supporters who are not parents, all rely on campaign volunteers asking community members if they will support the proposal. In successful campaigns, this is not a random contact program. Specific portions of the nonparent population are targeted for contact by the campaign. After election day, it is important to look at how well this population performed and, thereby, evaluate the effectiveness of the targeting used during the last campaign. Are identified supporters over- or underrepresented in the population that voted? What percentage of the total number of identified supporters cast ballots? As with the parent population, identified supporters may be overrepresented in the population that voted but the campaign may not be satisfied with the actual percentage casting ballots. Results can vary greatly. We have seen results ranging from a dismal 33% of supporters participating in the election up to an outstanding 95% of identified support casting ballots.

Especially when the potential in this population is not "maximized" on election day, analysis provides the needed data to craft a more-effective campaign plan. By looking at the gender, age, party affiliation, and geographic location of identified supporters, such an analysis allows the campaign to develop a clear picture of the individuals who failed to cast ballots. For example, if such an analysis reveals that all younger identified supporters who were Democrats with a weak long-term voting record failed to vote in the election, this fact will help the next campaign target its volunteer resources more effectively.

VOTING BY AREA

Surprising differences can be found when elections are compared. A postelection analysis completed for a Minnesota school district revealed that one part of the district only voted when the school placed a proposal on the ballot with a gubernatorial or presidential election. Like many school districts in the country, their school district boundaries are not contiguous with the city boundaries around them. The area of the district where the level of voter participation varied from election to election was part of a city identified with another school district. Without a vigorous effort to communicate with these voters, they would not understand that their votes made a difference to a school district they believed served another community. Since the postelection analysis for this district was completed as it prepared to place a proposal on the ballot with the election of the governor, district leaders modified their voter contact program to make sure these voters were provided with enough information to make it clear which school district served their neighborhoods—and which school district needed their votes.

Another example will help to emphasize this point. A number of campaigns have developed extensive plans to maximize the "yes" votes cast by recent school district graduates. These young voters are very often still registered in the community although they may be living on a college campus, on a military base, or in an apartment. They can usually be identified in the voter file by combining their age with the fact that they are still associated with a parent household due to the presence of a younger sibling. These campaigns often work very systematically with these young adults during the summer or at winter break to inform them of their vote's importance in the district's upcoming election. Postelection analysis of the votes cast by these younger voters will determine if this campaign tactic works. When it does, it should be included in the next campaign. When it does not, it should be replaced with a more effective tactic.

Finally, a postelection analysis should examine how the election compares with other recent elections. Too many school districts make the assumption that all elections are alike. They are not. Each election has a character that is defined by the types of candidates or issues that appear on the ballot. For example, a November election for governor or president will almost always attract a much younger, more male population than a primary, school board, or special election. The latter generally will attract a population that is older, more female, and more likely to vote in any election held in the area. Therefore, if the district just held a very successful school finance election on the ballot with the governor, do not assume it will be able to apply the same campaign plan to its next election if it is being held on a special election ballot.

One of the biggest differences among elections is the level of turnout. Despite all of the concern surrounding declining presidential election turnout during the last 50 years, a presidential election will attract the highest level of turnout in most communities. A gubernatorial election, if it appears on a different ballot, will attract the second highest level of voter turnout. There is generally a much lower level of voter participation in nominating primaries, city council, or school board elections. The lowest level of voter turnout usually occurs when there is a special election. These general election characteristics always need to be verified in the district. After looking at the differences in voter turnout, begin to look at differences in the demographic and geographic character of each type of election.

NOTE

Portions of this chapter were reprinted with permission from *The School Administrator*. Copyright 2003 American Association of School Administrators. All rights reserved.

1. This information is extremely important and is often poorly stored or discarded as soon as the polls have closed. Every election should generate an electronic file of its identified supporters containing sufficient information (e.g., name, address, phone number, and state voter identification number) to enable it to be easily linked to a new copy of the voter file used in a future election campaign.

CHAPTER 4

Mapping

If a picture is truly worth a thousand words, a good set of demographic maps is worth thousands of columns of numbers, counts, and statistics. Simply put, the statistics defining a school district can be made much easier to read and understand when they are visually displayed in a set of demographic maps. As part of the school finance election planning process, the results of the district's last finance election, the demographic characteristics of local voters, and U.S. Census data should be used to visually explore the nature and character of the district's neighborhoods and communities. The maps created as part of this process clearly and quickly allow school leaders to see the characteristics that may cause a proposal to be received in very different ways in various parts of the district.

This chapter examines three types of maps:

- *Election maps*. These maps extend the process of a postelection analysis. They are created from election results and the information contained in a fully annotated voter file.
- *U.S. Census data maps*. These maps build on election data by using information available from the U.S. Census to explore the demographic characteristics of the entire community.
- *Practical maps*. These maps help a campaign plan and execute parts of its voter contact program.

ELECTION MAPS

Precinct-by-precinct election results were not discussed as part of a postelection analysis. Precinct results can reveal whether support for the district's last proposal was uniform or whether support varied from neighborhood to neighborhood. If support was not uniform, it is very important to identify not only those areas where the proposal did very well but also those where it was soundly defeated. Most important, the district needs to identify those precincts where a few additional votes cast for or against the proposal would have changed the outcome of the vote at the precinct level.

To illustrate this discussion, the results of an election in which a school finance proposal won with 51.8% of the vote will be examined. Table 4.1 presents the precinct-by-precinct results as they were provided to the district after the election was certified by the local elections office. These results make it clear that the district's school finance proposal did extremely well in precincts such as Washington 3 and Lib-

Table 4.1. Precinct-by-Precinct Results

Precinct Name	Percentage "Yes"
Arnold	53.0
Deeds 1	54.3
Deeds 2	51.1
Douglas	54.1
Easttown	51.1
Edgerville 1	42.7
Edgerville 2	54.5
Edgerville 3	52.1
James 1	41.0
James 2	41.8
Liberty 1	51.3
Liberty 2	56.2
Liberty 3	53.4
Liberty 4	51.2
Lincoln 1	53.8
Lincoln 2	55.4
Madison 1	55.4
Madison 2	51.0
Madison 3	53.2
Madison 4	54.5
Madison 5	55.6
Upper James	50.1
Washington 1	53.7
Washington 2	42.1
Washington 3	58.3
Westboro	53.1
Wilderness	53.6

erty 2 where it won with more than 56% of the vote in each. These numbers also make it clear that in precincts James 1 and James 2 the district's proposal was beaten badly—winning only 41% of the vote. These numbers, however, reveal neither where these areas are located within the district nor anything about the voting and demographic characteristics of the people who live in these precincts. Mapping these results will allow the district to immediately see where these areas are located. By mapping additional data, the district gains a clear view of who these voters are and begins to understand why they voted against the school finance proposal.

Mapping precinct results reveals that three of the precincts that voted "no"—James 1, James 2, and Edgerville 1—are on the district's eastern end. The fourth, Washington 2, is in the south-central part of the district. On Map 4.1, these precincts are as depicted as black areas. There are also a number of precincts that create a band across the district from east to west where the proposal narrowly won or lost. These areas are identified on the map as shaded with diagonal lines. In the remainder of the district, the proposal did very well.

Understanding why the district's proposal did so poorly in these precincts begins by looking at other voter file data. Since this district had a fully annotated voter file available during its last election, the population of each precinct that is represented by parents who are registered to vote can be calculated. The results of these calculations can be used to create a map illustrating the areas of the district where parents represent a large percentage of the voting population and the areas where they represent a small percentage of the population registered to vote. A map using this information shows the four precincts where the district's proposal received its lowest level of support are also the areas where there is the lowest concentration of registered parents. The areas across the middle of the district where the outcome of the election was close are all areas where the parent population is neither a very large nor a very small percentage of the voting population. On Map 4.2, areas where the parents represent less than 10% of the registered voters in the precinct are printed in black. Areas where the parents represent more than 20% of the voting population are shaded gray with white stripes.

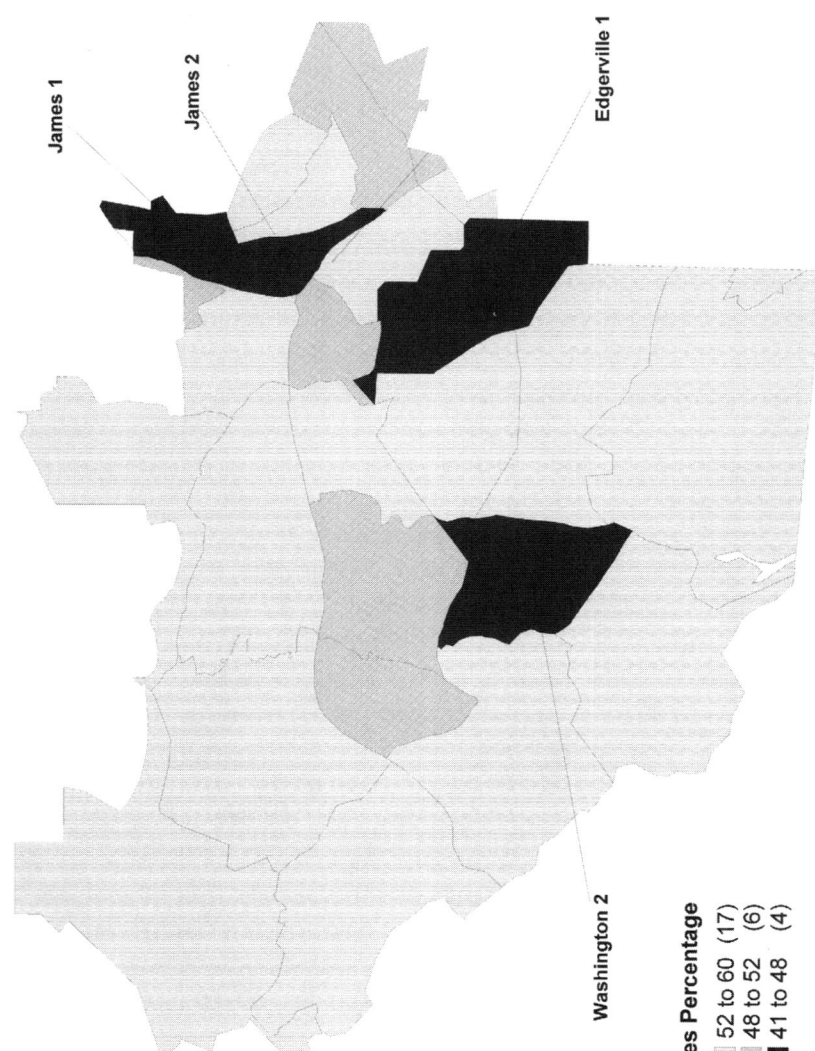

Map 4.1. "Yes" Percentage

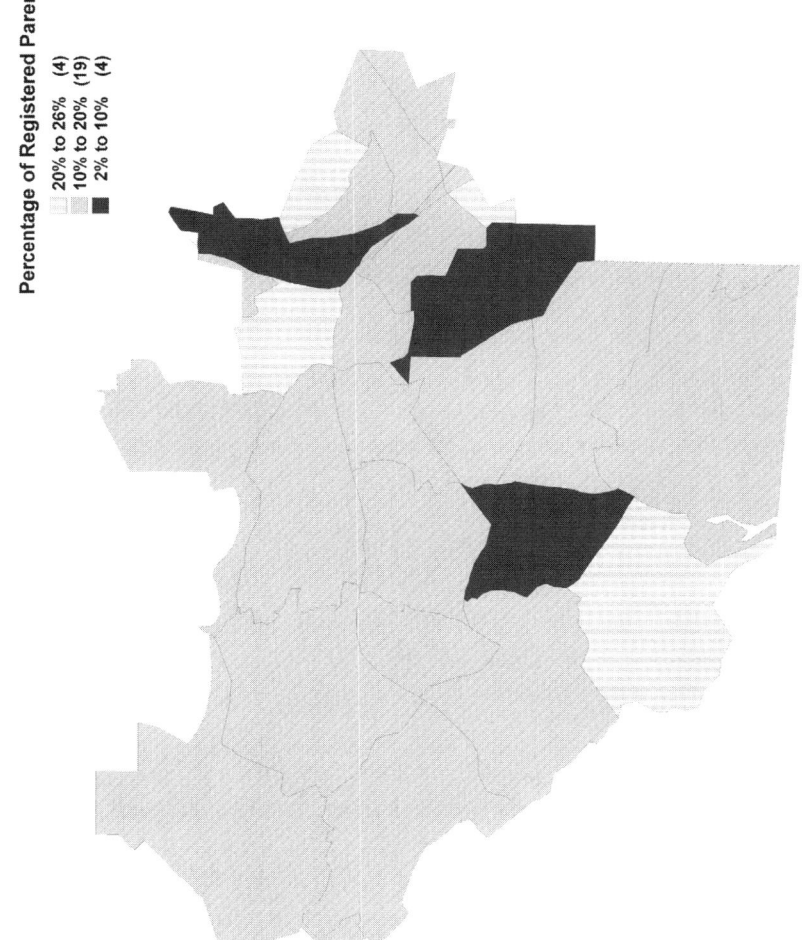

Map 4.2. Percentage of Registered Parents

Continuing to use the available voter file information, the district can look at the party affiliation of voters in each precinct.[1] On Map 4.3 each precinct is shaded based on the percentage of the voting population registered as Democrat. Although school finance proposals are not partisan proposals and receive support from all types of voters, it is generally true that voters who are affiliated with the Democratic Party are more likely to vote for a proposal than are their Republican neighbors. Therefore, knowing where the Democrats are concentrated will expand the campaign's understanding of the finance election's outcome. The areas printed in black are where Democrats make up less than 48% of the population of registered voters. There are five of these areas, and four are precincts in which the finance proposal received its lowest level of support. As a result, the district can begin to conclude that a lack of parents and a lack of Democrats may have made a difference in the way a precinct voted on the district's most recent proposal.

An additional type of map available to the campaign uses the classification of voters according to their past election activity discussed in Chapter 2. The classifications are:

- *Very Active Voters* are individuals who almost never miss an election.
- *Active Voters* are individuals who get to most elections.
- *Less Active or New Voters* are those individuals who either vote very infrequently or have recently registered to vote.

On Map 4.4, the percentage of the voting population in each precinct that consists of Very Active Voters has been used to illustrate where voting will be heaviest and lightest in any local election. The areas printed in black represent the areas in the district where Very Active Voters represent less than 10% of the voting population. The areas shaded with white stripes on a gray background are where more than 20% of the voting population is a Very Active Voter. The four precincts in which the district's school finance proposal received the lowest level of support are all precincts with a high percentage of Very Active Voters. This information expands our understanding of the voters in these precincts. It also tells the district that the attitudes of these voters will

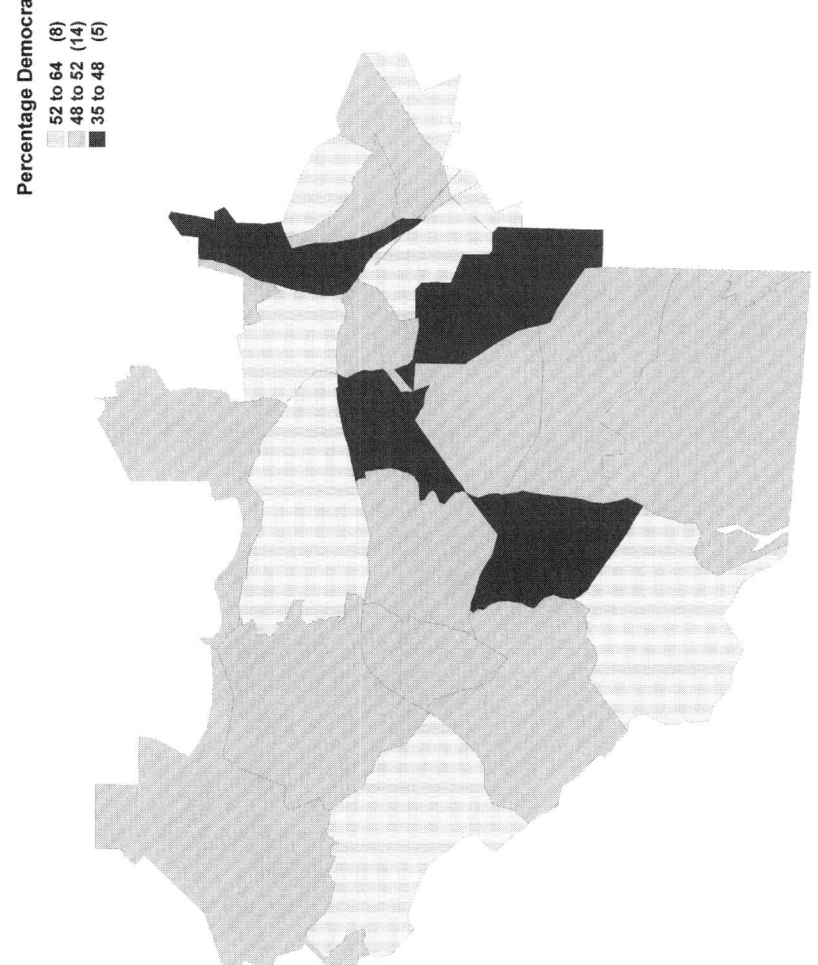

Map 4.3. *Percentage Democratic*

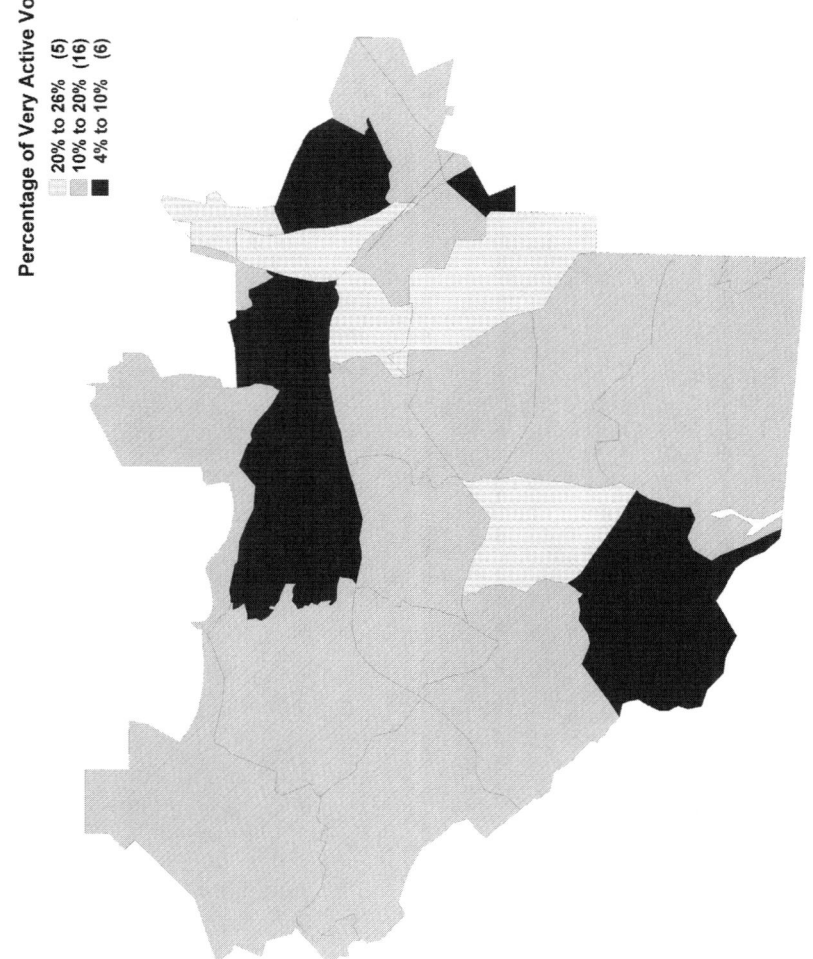

Map 4.4. Percentage of Very Active Voters

have an impact on any future district election. Because they are active voters and because they now have a history of voting against a local school finance proposal, the district may need to look for a way to build a better base of support among these individuals before its next election.

CENSUS DATA MAPS

To build a better base of support with the voters in the four precincts in which support for the last school finance proposal was weakest, it is important to learn more about these individuals. To do so, data from the U.S. Census can be mapped. The U.S. Census contains a vast amount of information about the residents of every community. The data can be mapped by using any of the geographic definitions developed for the census. In Maps 4.5, 4.6, and 4.7, data will be mapped into the census block groups contained inside the school district—beginning with age.

Map 4.5 illustrates the median age for each block group as measured by the 2000 census.[2] The areas printed in black represent areas where the median age is older than 50. There are four of these areas. One corresponds to Edgerville 1, which is one of the precincts in which the last school finance election fared very poorly. The other three are in precincts in which the proposal did well. Therefore, although age may be a factor in explaining why the last proposal did poorly in Edgerville 1, it is not the whole answer. Because there are areas in the district where older residents appear to have supported the school district, it may be possible for the district to find older supporters in those precincts who might be willing to help emphasize the importance of the schools to the older voters in Edgerville 1. An endorsement from other older voters might reduce the inclination of the residents of Edgerville 1 to oppose school taxes.

To continue to explore the district's demography, one can consult a map that illustrates the median household income in the block groups that make up the model school district. On Map 4.6, the areas printed in black represent the district areas where the median household income is lowest (i.e., less than $50,000 per year). The areas shaded in light gray represent areas where the median household income is highest

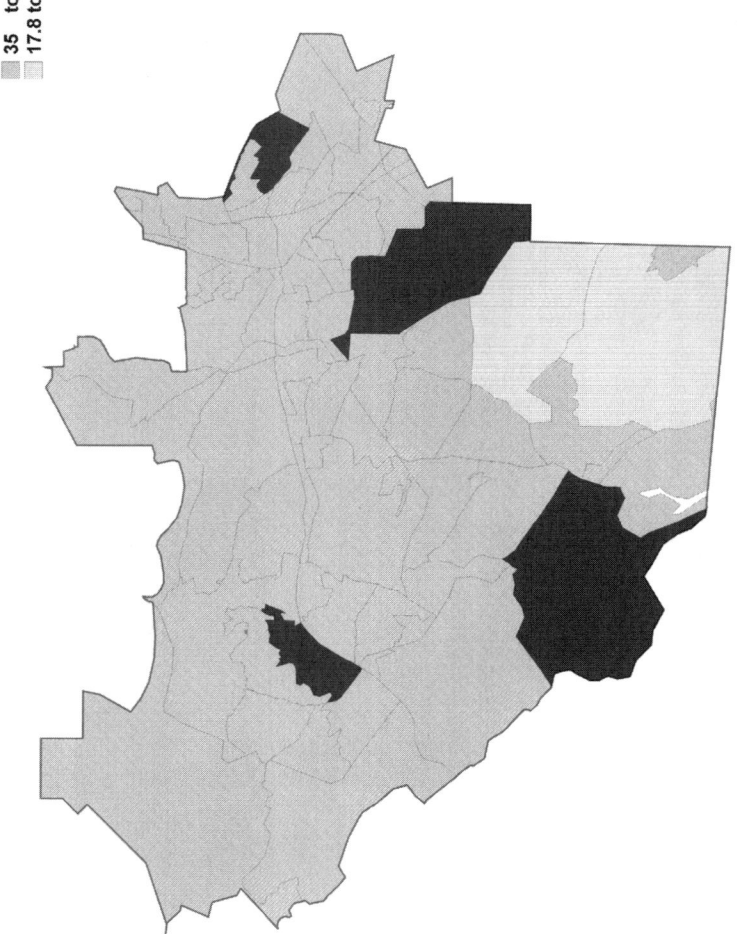

Map 4.5. Median Age

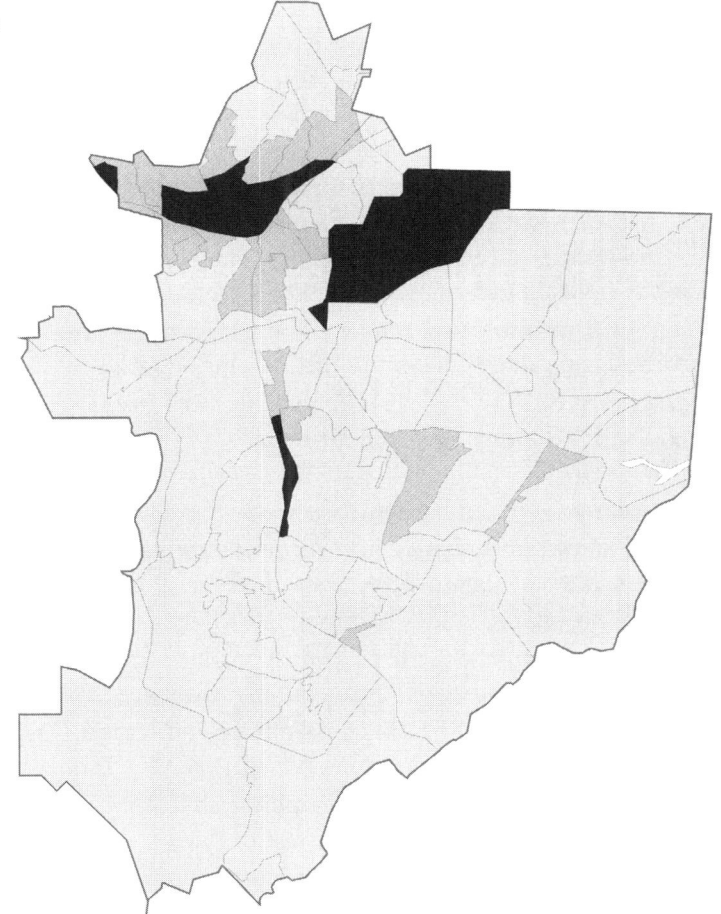

Map 4.6. *Median Household Income*

(i.e., from $76,000 to $295,000 per year). Three of the areas with a low median household income are contained in Edgerville 1, James 1, and James 2—precincts in which the school finance election did very poorly. Combining what was learned from this map and the map illustrating median age, it can be concluded that in Edgerville 1 the proposal did very poorly in part because older, less-affluent individuals populate the precinct. These individuals are also not Democrats or parents but vote all the time.

Finally, the district can map the median assessed value of homes in a district. Map 4.7 reveals that most of the district is very homogenous with most property assessed at more than $308,000. Two precincts, however, contain areas where the assessed value is much lower. The areas printed in black represent areas where the median assessed value of residential property is lowest (i.e., less than $204,000). The areas printed in darker gray represent block groups were the median assessed value is between $204,000 and $308,000. The areas where the median assessed value is less than $204,000 correspond to two of the precincts—Edgerville 1 and James 2—in which the district's proposal did poorly. Using these maps, the district can build a fairly complete demographic profile of the district residents who will represent the "toughest sell" when the next school finance proposal is placed on the ballot.

This discussion of demographic mapping started with the results of a previous school finance election and used maps created from voter file and U.S. Census data to learn more and more about the nature of the voters who opposed the last proposal. Maps using voter file and U.S. Census data can also be used to plan a future school finance election even when there are no results available from a previous election. In the maps created for this chapter from voter file and U.S. Census data, it was revealed that four precincts—Edgerville 1, James 1, James 2, and Washington 2—have demographic and voting characteristics that define them as different from the rest of the district. Even without a knowledge of how anyone in the district might vote on a proposal, a table summarizing the characteristics of its precincts allows the district to see the characteristics these four precincts have in common—characteristics that also define them as a region populated by individuals different from those in the rest of the district (see Table 4.2).

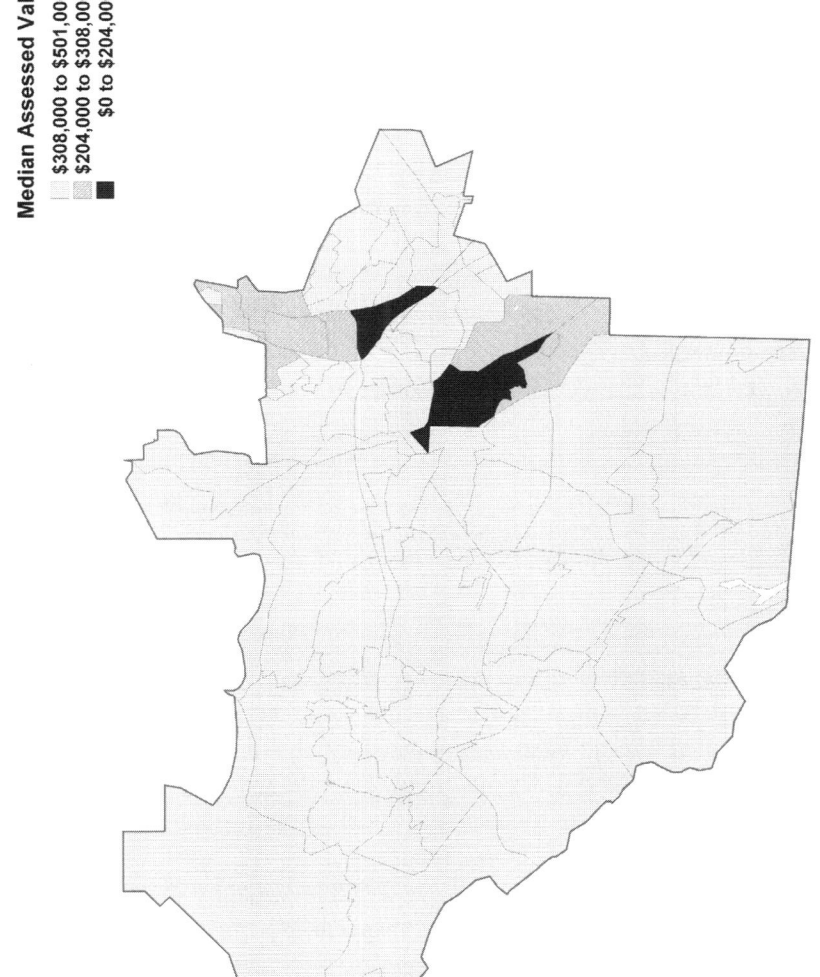

Map 4.7. Median Assessed Value

Table 4.2. District Precinct Characteristics

Precinct	Percent Parent	Percent Democrats	Percent Very Active	Median Age	Median Assessed Value	Median Household Income
James 1	Low	Low	High	Middle	Middle Range	Middle-to-Low Range
James 2	Low	Low	High	Middle	Middle-to- Range	Low Low
Edger. 1	Low	Low	High	High	Middle-to-Low	Low
Wash. 2	Low	Low	High	Middle	High Range	Middle-to-High

Knowing these regions exist before a community survey is completed will allow survey results to explore in detail regional differences in opinion concerning a school finance proposal. If the survey demonstrates that some of the areas with unique demographic characteristics also present a campaign with some unique challenges, plans can be developed to make sure these neighborhoods receive special attention from the campaign.

PRACTICAL MAPS

The maps discussed up to this point all allow the district to increase its knowledge of the whole district. They provide global pictures of the district's characteristics. "Practical maps," however, generally present detailed information about a precinct or a section of a precinct. They are used to help make sure everyone in the campaign knows how to find each polling place. In addition, they can be very useful as voter contact efforts—for example, a community walk, a "dear friend" campaign,[3] or a get-out-the-vote drive—are planned.

The simplest practical map illustrates where the polling place will be in each precinct. Such maps can be very useful as volunteers work to ensure voters know where to go on election day. Because they simply provide information and do not advocate for a "yes" or "no" vote, these maps can also be posted at school where parents and teachers can use them to help get voters to the ballot box. Map 4.8 illustrates this type of practical map.

This type of map can also be an effective planning tool for campaign activities. Many campaigns include a community walk during which volunteers go door to door to contact likely supporters who cannot be reached by phone. To plan this type of walk, a precinct map depicting where these voters live can be very useful. Map 4.9 places a little flag at each address where an uncontacted, registered parent lives. As street names are not assigned in alphabetical order, those charged with the task of planning a walk to these houses can use such a map to group streets that are connected and close together. A similar map could be created showing where all the identified "yes" voters live in the precinct. As a campaign plans its get-out-the-vote drive, such a map would allow it to determine in advance the best way for every "yes" voter to get to the polls on election day.

Campaign volunteers can also decide whether it is practical to walk to all the parent doors in the precinct. Map 4.10 zooms into one corner of the precinct. It is clear that a door-to-door walk on Ruppel Place could be very productive while there will be no need to walk down Rohrer Drive. The level of detail that can be achieved on such a planning map can be increased tremendously.

The last sample map in this chapter examines one city block. On Map 4.11, homes shaded gray are the homes of public school parents. The presence of a gray dot indicates the presence of a registered parent. A black dot represents a registered parent who voted in the last election. It is also possible to map the houses on a street where parents live and then differentiate the houses in which the parents are Very Active Voters from those in which the parents are Less Active or New Voters. The latter may miss the district's next school finance election and would make good targets for a "dear friend" postcard or a knock on the door to remind them to vote. If information is added to the map so that it can also show where unregistered parents live, an effective, highly targeted voter registration effort can be planned and executed.

Map 4.8. Polling Place

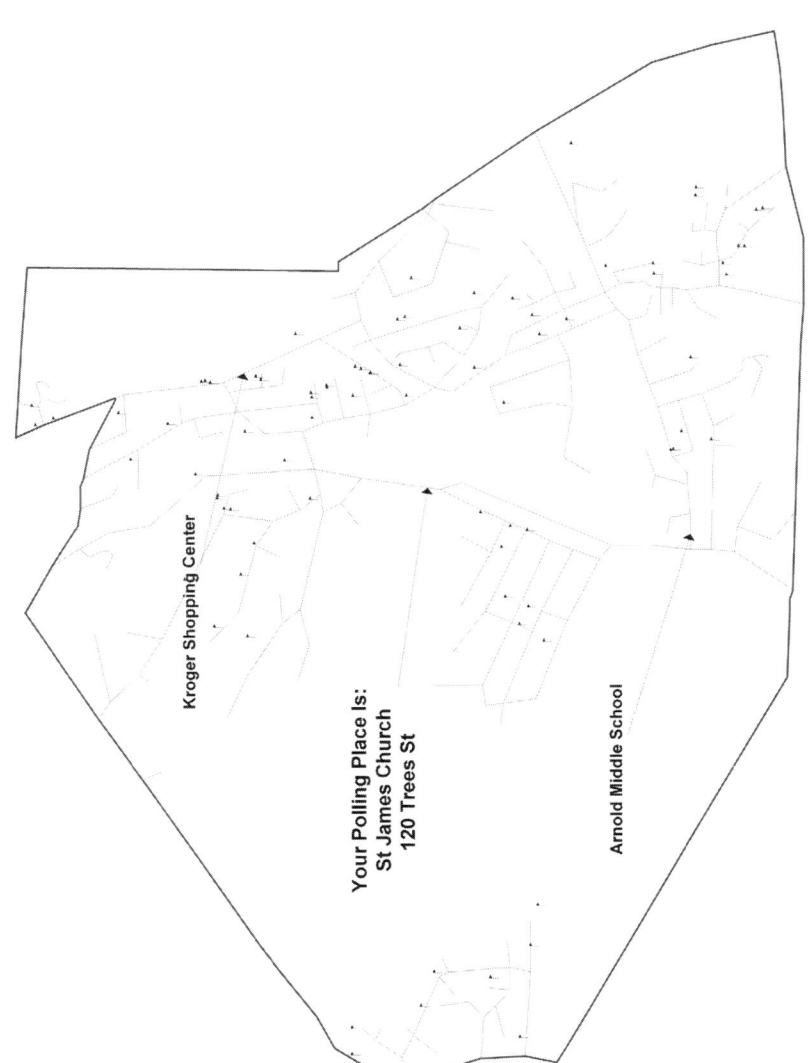

Map 4.9. *Voter Contact*

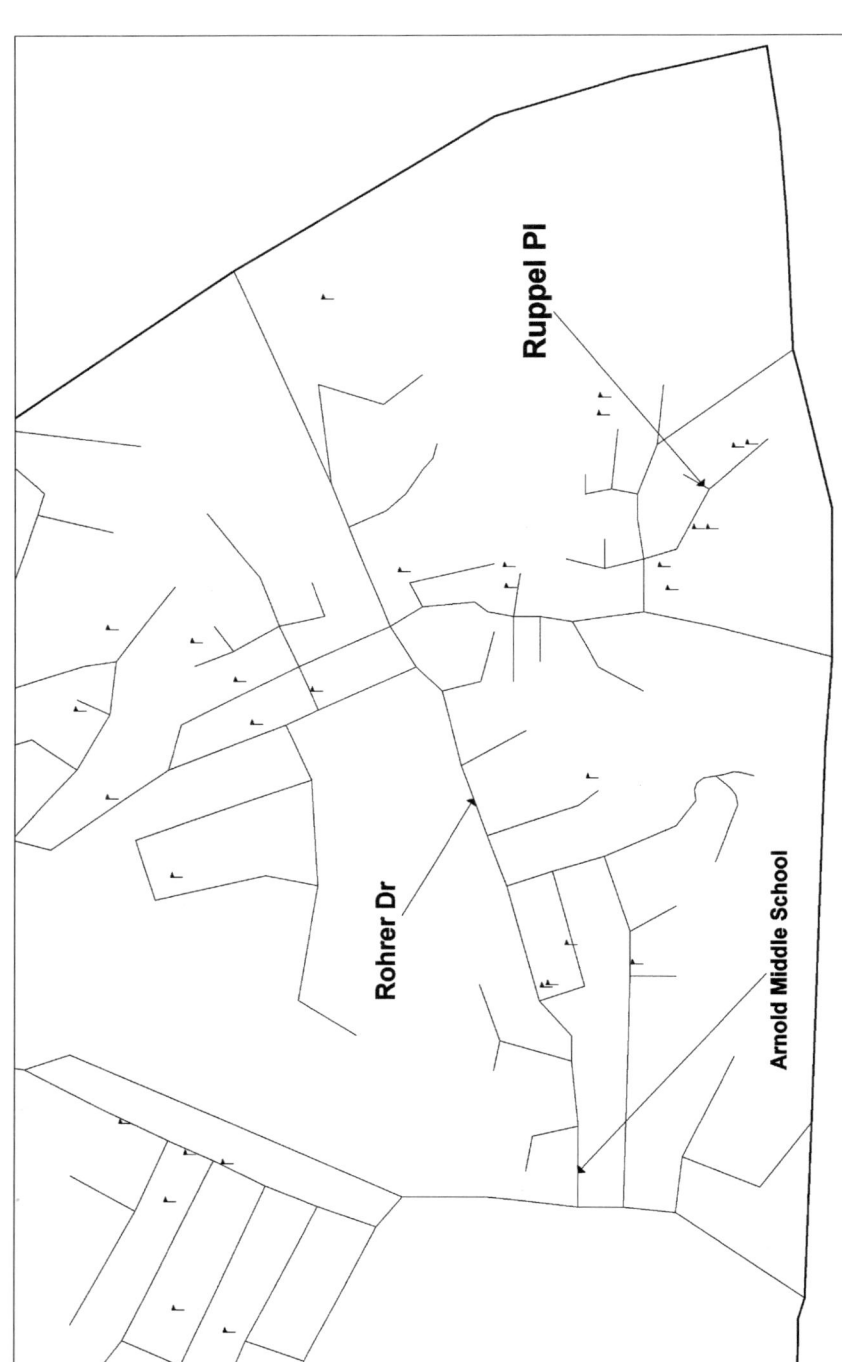

Map 4.10. Door-to-Door

602	601	600	601	311	601
608	609	604	611	610	609
614	615	608		612	613
	619	612	617	618	619
620	623	616	621	620	
624	625	620	625	624	625
632	629	624	629	632	629
	633	632	637	636	631
636	637	640	641	640	637
644	645	644			645
648	649	648	649	648	651
658	657	656	655	658	657

Map 4.11. Single City Block

NOTES

1. In many states, voters do not register by party. In those states, you can use precinct level results for minor statewide offices to identify the partisan character of a precinct. (Note: Minor statewide offices are those elected positions that never seem to attract a lot of media attention and in which the candidates involved are not well known even by election day. In fact, in many of these races only the candidate's immediate family really knows for whom they are voting.)

2. Very good annual U.S. Census updates are also available. These can be purchased from commercial data companies such as Claritas or, in some cases, obtained from local planning offices. These updates are essential when mapping data five or six years after the U.S. Census was taken.

3. To conduct a "dear friend" campaign, campaign volunteers handwrite postcards to supportive voters in their neighborhoods who might forget to vote when the district has a school finance proposal on the ballot.

CHAPTER 5

Community Survey

A community survey is a scientific measurement of voter opinion at a specific moment in time that is designed to determine if it is feasible to place a school finance proposal on the ballot. If it is feasible, the survey determines how much the community is willing to increase local taxes for the benefit of the schools. In addition, such a survey functions as an assessment of the school district's performance and should explore the community's perception of the overall quality of the education being provided to local children; the ability of the district to manage its budget; and the degree to which voters believe the district spends tax dollars wisely. In most states, school districts are allowed to commission and pay for such a survey as part of the school finance election preparation process. In every election, it is essential that a community survey be completed before a proposal is placed on the ballot.

THE BASICS: WHO?

Every school finance election survey should be based on interviews with registered voters.[1] In every community, the most active registered voters in the school district will have a very strong influence on the success or failure of any proposal placed on the ballot. Therefore, understanding how these voters react to a proposal is extremely important. When a community survey is based on interviews with registered voters, it extends the demographic knowledge gained by reading the count book produced from the contents of the district's voter file. Likewise,

> **IMPORTANT TERMS**
>
> The following terms are used in this chapter and may be unfamiliar.
>
> - *Cross-tabulation*, which means dividing the responses according to the demographic characteristics of the individuals being interviewed. These are often called "cross-tabs." The simplest is the cross-tab by gender that allows one to look at the response among male voters separated from the response among female voters.
> - *Uninformed benchmark* is a question included in surveys before information is presented to those being interviewed about the need for and cost of a district's proposal.
> - *Informed benchmark* is a question included in the survey after information has been presented to those being interviewed.
> - *Margin of error* is a measure of the accuracy of the results of the survey.
> - *Sample* is the list of individuals who may be asked to complete an interview as part of the survey process. These individuals are selected at random from all of the voters in the district.
> - *Sample size* is the number of completed interviews used as the basis for a survey.

it adds depth to the understanding developed about voter behavior by a postelection analysis. But a community survey achieves these goals only if it is based on interviews with registered voters.

But saying that a survey will be based on interviews with registered voters does not answer all of the questions involved in deciding *who* should be interviewed. There are a number of ways to design the sample for such a community survey. All have been used to plan successful school finance elections, but each has some distinct strengths and weaknesses.

Some pollsters like to survey only the most active voters in the community. Using the definitions developed in the discussion of the voter file in Chapter 2, they design a sample that will cause all of the interviews to be completed with Very Active Voters. Because these voters will have a major impact on any election held in the district, this approach will produce the safest recommendations for the district. But this approach may also provide the district with recommendations that raise a minimal amount of money since the most active voters in most districts are older voters without school-age children.

Other pollsters interview only the voters that they think will participate in an election scheduled for the next date available for a proposal. This approach produces recommendations that are extremely accurate as long as the assumptions made about who will probably vote in the next election are not changed by events that occur between the execution of the survey and election day. If events do force a change in those assumptions, the results of such a survey may not provide as much insight into the impact of those changes or allow the district to effectively explore the feasibility of placing a proposal on any of the other election dates available in the future.

Finally, there are pollsters who design their surveys so that they conduct interviews with voters of all types after excluding individuals from the sample who have died, moved, or stopped voting. This type of survey will produce the most complete picture of community reaction to a school finance election and allow the district to look at a full range of financial recommendations. Cross-tabulation is used to explore the reaction of the Very Active Voters in the district and to explore the support available from those most likely to vote in the next election. If there is little or no support for a tax increase among the most active voters in the community or among the voters most likely to participate in the next available election date, a more complete picture of voter opinion will allow the district to assess the benefits and risks involved with a proposal that must depend on voters who will need to be vigorously reminded to vote if the proposal is to succeed. The disadvantage of this type of survey is that the margin of error among many of the groups of voters interviewed is often higher.

THE BASICS: HOW MANY?

A community survey does not involve calls to all voters in the district. In fact, these surveys are based on interviews with a relatively small number of registered voters. Deciding how many interviews to complete as part of a community survey depends on two factors. The first relates to the fact that the primary goal of the survey is to measure overall community opinion with a sufficient level of precision to predict the feasibility of a school finance election. The level of precision or the margin of error in any survey is determined by a formula that is based on the total number of interviews completed for the survey. It does not depend on the total number of registered voters in the school district. As noted by Celina Lake, "A sample of 200 from a congressional district has the same error rate as a sample of 200 drawn from the United States" (Lake & Callbeck, 1987). Therefore, we recommend a community survey be based on a minimum of 300 interviews, achieving a margin of error of +/− 5.5% with a 95% confidence level. In general, sample sizes tend to range from 300 to 600 interviews. Such surveys present results where the margin of error is +/− 5.5% for 300 interviews to +/− 4% for 600 interviews. This level of precision is sufficient to plan a successful school finance election.[2]

The second factor applies in districts with large voting populations and in which the results of a postelection analysis or demographic mapping have made it clear that the survey should also be designed to accurately measure regional differences of opinion. In such cases, the sample size might be increased to 800 or 1,000 to increase the level of precision in each region of the district.

An example will illustrate how this is done. A suburban high school district in California's San Francisco Bay Area is home to 70,000 voters in three distinct communities. One is composed of three small suburb cities where incomes and home values are significantly higher than in the rest of the district. The second is a larger suburban community that has a more diverse mixture of income levels and ethnic groups. It also includes a well-developed downtown business section in addition to residential neighborhoods. The third area is a large retirement community where all residents must be older than 55 and no children are allowed. The results of postelection analysis and mapping clearly differentiate among these regions.

To ensure a survey can accurately measure differences of opinion concerning a school tax in each of these areas, the sample size in the district is increased to 800. Completing this number of interviews increases the overall precision of the survey. More important, it allows the survey to include enough interviews in each region that the margin of error for each area is sufficient to allow opinion in the more upscale suburbs to be compared to opinion in the larger community. Opinion in both areas can then be compared with the reaction of the retirement community to a school finance election.

There are practical limits, however, to increasing the sample size in a community survey for a school district. Some districts are just too small. If there are only 2,500 to 3,500 voters in the district, it is not necessary—or practical—to complete more than 300 interviews. In districts with fewer than 20,000 voters, it may not be practical to complete more than 400 interviews. Attempting to do so will simply become disruptive and the persistence of the interview team could potentially anger local voters.

THE BASICS: HOW?

The interviews completed as a part of the surveys are done via telephone. The phone has one major advantage over surveys completed through the mail or over the Internet. Before the first interview begins, the information in the count book has defined the demography of the district's voting population. As telephone interviews are completed, the demography of the interviewees is carefully monitored and adjustments are made to the selection of phone numbers from the sample to ensure the population interviewed has the same demographic characteristics as the population of voters in the district. If one is trying to interview through the mail or over the Internet, one can only hope that all demographic groups will respond.[3]

There is a secondary reason for relying on the telephone to complete the interviews required for a community survey. The telephone will be the primary means by which a campaign in support of a school finance election makes contact with local voters. If the survey can use the telephone to complete a set of interviews and the results of the interviews demonstrate it is feasible to place a proposal on the ballot and expect to win, the campaign in support of that proposal can also expect to use the phone to identify enough support to win on election day.

THE BASICS: WHEN?

The timing of a community survey is a compromise between a desire to collect survey results as close to election day as possible and the need to use those results to plan and shape the district's proposal. In an ideal world, a district would execute a survey a few days before it had to place a school finance proposal on the ballot and have the results back just before the school board votes to call the election. The survey's results would reflect the attitudes of the voters in the district in an economic and political environment that would probably not change significantly before election day. Unfortunately, completing a survey just before the district must call an election does not allow the district to use the results to shape the proposal, plan the presentation of the proposal to the community, or thoughtfully assess the strengths and weaknesses of the projects to be funded by the school finance election. Therefore, community surveys are generally completed three to six months before the district must act to call an election. Timing the survey in this way affords the district enough time to react to all the survey's information. Most importantly, the district can ensure the tax increase–funded projects align well with the attitudes and opinions of local voters.

There are also times when a district will plan for two surveys. This approach allows an initial survey to be completed 10 to 12 months before the district must act. These early surveys are usually used to explore the possible ways in which tax funds will be used so projects can be developed in alignment with community opinion. An early survey will also identify projects that are out of alignment and require extensive community discussion if voters are to understand why and how these projects are important to the district's health and strength. Early surveys are also useful in districts in which recent events make it clear that local voters may have a less-than-positive opinion of the district's ability to plan or spend tax dollars wisely. By exploring voter opinion 10 to 12 months before the district must call an election, a communications plan can be developed addressing concerns among local voters about the district's fiscal skills and overall performance. If an early survey is completed, a second (shorter) survey is generally planned just a few weeks or months before the district must place a proposal on the ballot. This survey will retest tax tolerance and assess the impact of any communication with local voters undertaken as a result of the first survey.

THE QUESTIONNAIRE

The community survey's questionnaire needs to test the impact of information about the district's school finance proposal on the level of support available in the community. School finance elections are different from all other elections because the only thing that can motivate an individual to vote to give away money is information about *why* the district needs the money. Other elections—even other referenda—do not have the kind of direct, immediate impact on household budgets that one finds in a school finance election. In a candidate race, many voters will make up their mind as soon as they find out the candidate is a Republican or a Democrat—or, in the case of the 2003 California gubernatorial recall election, an actor lacking political experience. In a school finance election, the only party that exists is the uninformed party—voters intent on voting "no" because they do not know anything about the proposal. Without information, voters will vote "no." To understand clearly what information prevents this reaction and persuades voters to cast a "yes" vote, a community survey must test the impact of presenting voters with more and more information about the tax proposal.

The first step in the interview, therefore, is to ask everyone if they favor or oppose the district's proposal before any detailed information is presented. For a bond election, the question might read as follows: "The Brisbane Elementary School District may place a bond measure on the ballot that would increase property taxes to raise the funds needed to renovate the district's schools and classrooms. Would you favor or oppose such a proposal?" When the survey is designed to explore a tax increase to raise operating funds, the question might read: "The Stillwater Area Public Schools may ask local voters to approve an increase in local property taxes to provide the district with the funds needed to avoid budget cuts, the elimination of teaching positions, and an increase in class size. Would you favor or oppose such a proposal?"

This question is referred to as the *uninformed benchmark* (see Figure 5.1). As these examples illustrate, the questions provide very few details about the proposal. The interviewee knows it involves an increase in local taxes. But the question does not present any information about the cost of the proposal to the individual being interviewed. The possible uses of the funds raised by this proposal are described only in general terms. The purpose is to identify those voters who will support virtually anything the district places on the ballot. Knowing how large this population is tells the district the size and demographic character of the base of support for its proposal.

Once the uninformed benchmark has been asked, details about the district's proposal are presented. These questions attempt to break the whole proposal into its smallest component parts and test each part separately. Therefore, instead of following the uninformed benchmark with a four- or five-sentence statement describing the need for the school finance proposal, each of the ideas that might be included in

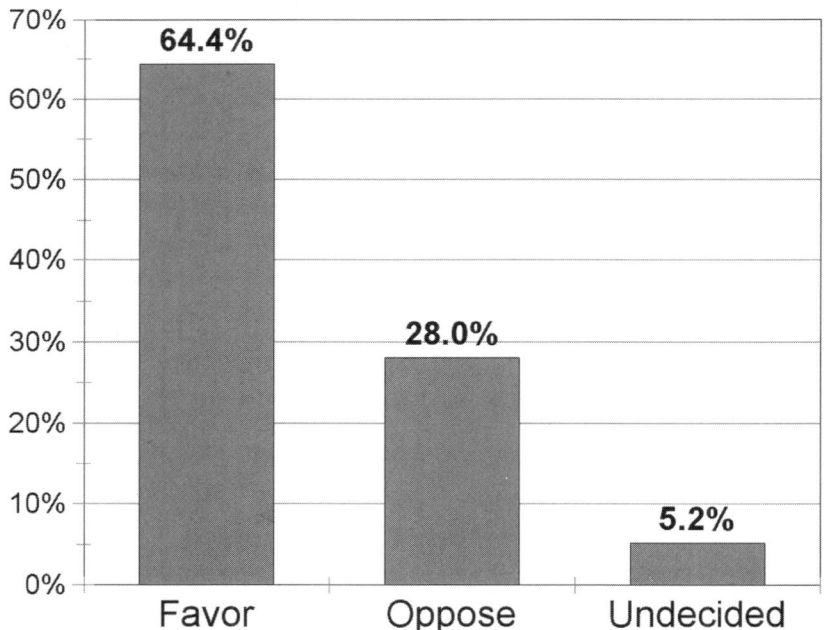

Figure 5.1. **The Uninformed Benchmark**

such a short statement are presented in separate questions to see how voters react to each individual statement. Therefore, in the following example, instead of stating that funds will be used to restore both the music program and physical education program, two questions are presented. The first reads: "Funds will be used to restore reductions made in the music program." The second probes for a reaction to the idea that "funds will be used to restore reductions made in the physical education program."

For a bond, separate questions would be used to explore voter reaction to the use of bond funds to replace plumbing, upgrade electrical systems, and install new energy-efficient heating systems. This approach produces results allowing the district to clearly see which parts of an argument favoring the school finance proposal cause voters to become more likely to support it and which do not. Responses to questions presenting information about the school finance proposal are ranked according to the number of people made more likely to support the proposal by the information presented (see Table 5.1).

Table 5.1. Community Survey Questions

Percent More Likely	Statement
72.7	10. Leaks in the aging water system are common. One recently resulted in the flooding of a school library.
67.9	16. Funds will be used to replace the 40-year-old gas lines at the public schools.
65.8	9A. Funds will be used to replace the 40-year-old water lines at the public schools.
65.5	12. Funds will be used to create an energy management system that will make the heating and cooling of all district buildings more energy efficient.
65.3	14. Funds will be used to provide expanded libraries and media centers at all schools.
60.0	15. An independent oversight committee will ensure funds are spent responsibly and according to the district's board-approved plan.
59.2	11. Funds will be used to improve student safety at drop-off areas and in parking lots.
57.4	8. Funds will be used to replace existing 40-year-old single-pane classroom windows with more energy-efficient windows.
56.0	13. Funds will be used to replace portable classrooms with permanent classrooms.

The types of statements tested in most surveys fall into a few well-defined categories. A survey should test

- information about the situation that makes it necessary for the district to consider a school finance proposal.
- information about the ways in which the funds raised by the tax will be spent.
- information about the consequences of not raising additional funds through a tax increase.
- information about the structure and features of the school finance proposal itself.

Some surveys will also test a number of negative statements about the school finance proposal. Such a statement would read: "With all the uncertainty about the economy right now, it's just not a good time to be raising taxes." The responses to this type of question produce a picture of who will react—and how severely—if someone attacks the district's proposal. Although often useful to the planning of a school finance campaign, negative questions should be included in the survey only if there is room in the instrument after consideration and inclusion of all possible positive statements. If the budget limits the length of the questionnaire, do not use up space with questions probing possible negative statements.

Once all of the statements about the proposal have been presented, everyone is asked again if they would favor or oppose the proposed measure. This question is called the *informed benchmark*. The responses to this question allow us to see if information has increased support for the proposal (see Figure 5.2).

If support increases at this point in the survey, the individual items presented need to be ranked to see which items had the greatest impact. The statements that made the largest number of people more likely to vote for the proposal will form the core of the school finance proposal presentation to the community. If, on the other hand, support does not increase—or worse, goes down—the individual items described in the survey will need to be carefully evaluated to determine the reason.[4] By

"WORDSMITHING" WITH SPLIT SAMPLE QUESTIONS

In addition to exploring voter reaction to the projects and programs that might be funded by a tax increase, split sample questions explore voter reaction to the words chosen to describe those projects and programs. Interviewees are divided into two equal groups. Half of them are presented with one version of a question. The other half are presented with a version of the same question in which key words or phrases have been changed.

For example, a survey was done for a district that wanted to use bond funds to create what its administrators called "high-school parent/student centers." When asked, people at the district could explain that these were areas proposed for use as tutoring centers. They called them "parent/student centers" because they expected parents to be among the volunteers coming to the centers to help tutor students. The name "parent/student center" had become so attached to this project that district leaders had started writing it into communications material intended for the entire community. We decided that we needed to test the impact of using this language before proceeding further with such communications materials. To do so, half of those interviewed were asked if knowing that "funds will be used to create parent/student centers at local high schools" made them more or less likely to support the district's bond proposal. The other half were presented with a question that read: "Funds will be used to create areas at the high schools where parents and other volunteers can tutor students." The results made it clear that referring to "parent/student centers" did not convey enough meaning to the voters in the community. Less than half (or 49%) were made more likely to vote for the bond by this information. An explanation that these were tutoring centers made 60% more likely to vote "yes." As the campaign progressed, the district was able to avoid the use of its own jargon during the campaign and more clearly explain the purpose of this expenditure.

doing so, the district can better align its needs to the community's appetite for additional school projects.

Analyzing the overall results of the uninformed and informed benchmark questions is only the first step, however, in the process of understanding the data collected in a community survey. The cross-tabulation of

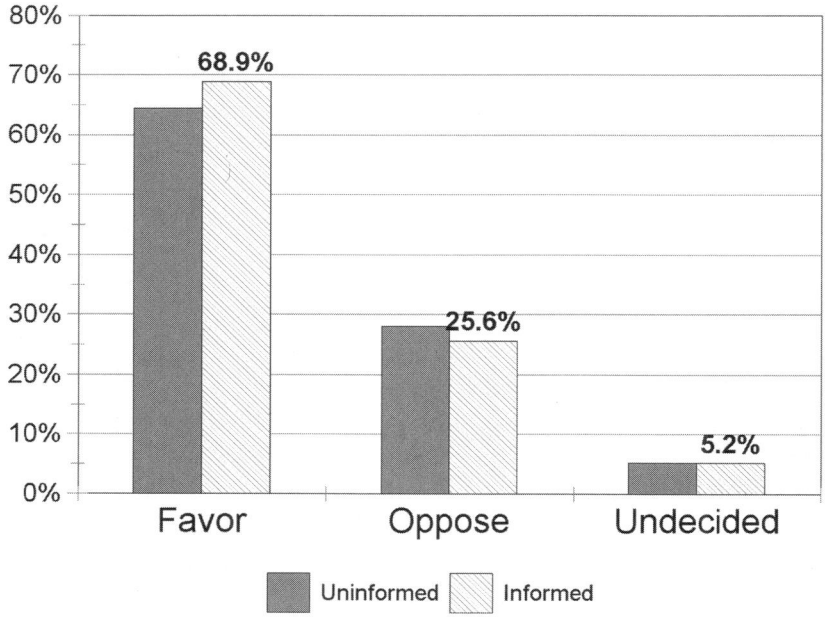

Figure 5.2. The Informed Benchmark

this data by the demographic characteristics of the voters interviewed greatly expands our understanding of the responses. By cross-tabulating survey results, the district learns if men and women are equally supportive of the proposal or if older voters show the same level of support as younger voters.

The demographic characteristics of the voters come from two sources. Some are collected as the interviewees answer specific survey questions. For example, each person interviewed is asked if he or she has school-age children in the household. If they do, the individual can then be asked if the children in the household go to public or private school. Based on each individual's responses to these questions, the responses to the benchmark questions can be divided according to "parent status" (see Figure 5.3). This is the *asked demography* developed in the survey. It is available because a question was included in the questionnaire that collected information about the interviewee. Other examples of asked demography might include

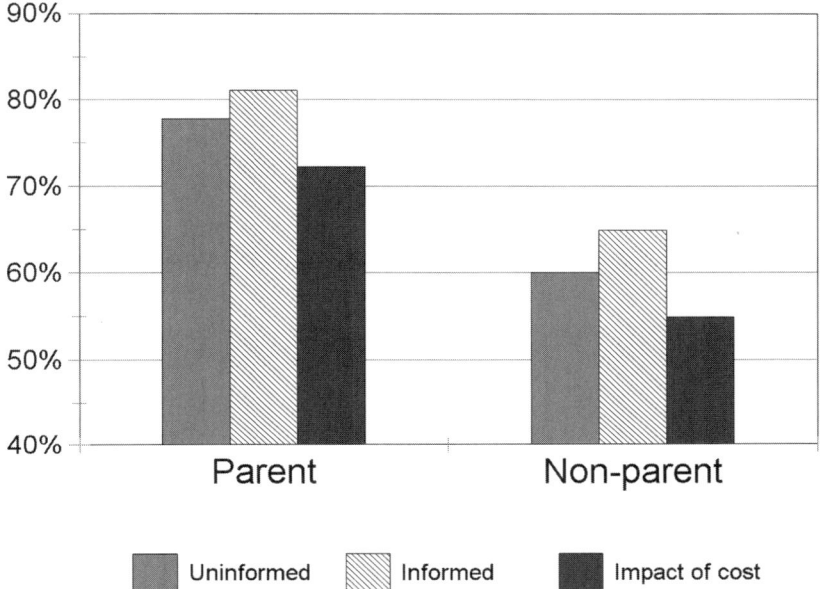

Figure 5.3. A Parent Cross-Tabulation

questions about household income, the highest level of education attained by interviewee, ethic or religious background, and employment status.

The voter file also contains demography available for cross-tabulation. This information is *file demography*. It includes information about the interviewee's voting activity, his or her voter registration date, and where he or she lives. The cross-tabulations completed from file demography are generally the most important to the successful planning and execution of a school finance election.[5] Although it may be interesting to use the results of an asked question about income to cross-tabulate the responses according to high- and low-income voters, in most school finance election campaigns there is no immediate way to put this information to work. Voter files do not contain information about the income level of individual voters so to begin using the results of a cross-tabulation on income, one must find a way to identify high- and low-income neighborhoods in the district. Demographic mapping provides some of the necessary information but file demography is immediately useable. It allows the district to immediately use the results of the cross-tabulation to produce lists of voters who will be the most supportive of the district's proposal.

EXPLORING REACTIONS TO COST

Up to this point, the survey has explored the impact of information about the benefits of or need for the tax dollars to be raised by the district's proposal. The next step is to explore the impact of cost information on the base of support created by this information. The questions that complete this task are the *tax tolerance questions* that need to be included in each survey.

There are a number of ways to accurately measure community tax tolerance. The key to producing an accurate result, however, is the fact that voters will react best to a cost that specifically relates to how much money the proposal will remove from their household budgets. Therefore, to determine whether local voters will support a $30 million school bond, one does not ask voters whether they would prefer a $20 million, $25 million, $30 million, or $40 million bond. Numbers like these are too large for voters to relate to their day-to-day expenses. After all, no one being interviewed will be asked to pay the entire cost of the bond. Nor can we expect them to have any detailed knowledge of how much it might cost to build a new school or renovate their neighborhood's middle school. Therefore, a survey should present numbers that describe the average annual cost of a $30 million bond and ask voters to react to these numbers. This presentation should be made in terms of the cost of the bond to the average homeowner or the cost in terms of the average assessed value of a home in the community. The survey's results will provide the district with an optimal annual cost to the average district homeowner. The district's financial advisors will use this number to calculate the amount of money the district can raise for building or renovation.[6]

> **ONE TEST IS NOT ENOUGH**
>
> Assessing tax tolerance usually requires that two types of questions be included in a survey. The first type presents a very specific cost to those being interviewed after they have heard information about the need for a tax increase. Such specific cost questions generally read as follows: "I want to add one additional fact. If you knew that the proposed school bond would have an average annual cost of $30 per $100,000 of assessed value, would you favor or oppose this proposal?" At another place in the questionnaire, voters are also asked to react to three to five other possible costs for the school finance proposal. The responses to these questions develop a trend line that allows the district to see how support decreases as cost increases. This trend line can be used to project an acceptable tax rate if the response to the presentation of a specific cost fails to achieve sufficient support.

HOW ARE WE DOING?

At this point, the survey has collected enough information to know whether a school finance election is feasible, to identify the projects that best align with community opinion, and to determine an acceptable cost for the proposal. There is one more area that should be explored in every survey: how the community perceives the district. Survey questions explore how voters rate the overall quality of the education provided by the district as well as how they evaluate the performance of teachers, principals, the superintendent, and the school board. In addition, voters should be asked to assess the job the district is doing in spending local tax dollars and managing its budget. These questions develop a profile of the district that adds depth to the knowledge gained by testing voter reaction to specific facts about the district's proposal. This profile is extremely important in the planning of a successful school finance campaign. If too many voters have a negative opinion of the district's performance—especially its fiscal capability—it will be extremely difficult to win community approval for any proposal (Lifto & Morris, 2000). Knowing this type of information while planning a school finance election is much more useful than finding it out in the middle of a campaign launched to support a school finance proposal.

HOW ABOUT A FOCUS GROUP?

Focus groups are often used in planning a school finance election. A focus group brings together a random sample of voters—usually selected from a group that may present a challenge to the approval of a local school tax increase. The participants in a focus group are usually presented with the best argument the district believes it can make for its proposal. The focus group participants are encouraged to question, discuss, and interact with each other concerning the content of the presentation. As they are doing so, focus group participants are observed and careful notes made concerning the items in the presentation to which they react very positively or very negatively. A focus group produces more subjective information than does the community survey. Used together, they can enable a district to develop a strong, persuasive message for use during the campaign communications program.

NOTES

1. Even in states that allow for same-day voter registration, the known registered voters in the community are ready (and in many cases eager) to cast a ballot in any election held in the district. To plan successfully, a district must understand how these voters will react to a tax proposal.

2. The American Research Group provides a handy margin-of-error calculator at www.americanresearchgroup.com/moe.html.

3. This conclusion reflects the status of interviewing by phone, mail, or Internet when this chapter was written. The ability of the Internet to serve as a medium for interviewing is evolving on a daily basis. It will most likely become a more useful interviewing tool in the future.

4. Some projects almost always test poorly. These include bond proposals to build athletic facilities, administrative offices, or swimming pools as well as operating proposals to restore administrative positions lost at the district office.

5. This is true in those districts that must rely on direct mail, the telephone, and the community's one local newspaper or radio station to communicate with local voters. The results of asked demography become more useful in very large districts in which paying for media space or time requires careful demographic planning. If a campaign is faced with a media market with multiple outlets, it must decide which radio and television stations or newspapers are the best places for the district's message. In such cases, all of the demography developed during the survey will be extremely valuable.

6. In addition, most tax tolerance tests are made in terms of the cost per year. Doing so usually aligns the costs being presented in the survey with the costs that will be presented in the legal documents that must appear on the ballot with a local school finance proposal.

CHAPTER 6
Ballot Questions

Crafting an effective ballot question traditionally encompasses three dimensions: content, cost, and structure. In light of the ballot question's central role in election day success, aligning it with a community's values *and* willingness to pay become key policy decisions for the school board. Although states vary in terms of how much ballot structure and language flexibility is extended to school districts, school leaders must use available data to determine the community's tax-cost threshold prior to shaping the ballot question. Scientific survey results and the count book position school leaders to respond to the content, cost, and structure dimensions, providing the school district and proponents with a sound foundation from which to campaign.

CONTENT

Simply put, the content is the "what" of the district's proposal. Is it a new middle school? A new high school? Reduced class sizes? Expanded Advanced Placement courses? Regardless, the research is clear—districts that scientifically test voters' preferences and design ballot questions reflecting the community's values are more likely to prevail on election day. As described in Chapter 5, a well-designed scientific survey is a prerequisite to achieving alignment, both in terms of the "big" question (e.g., a new high school or reduced class sizes) as well as specific elements of the proposal. Safety improvements may be a top priority in one community while voters in another school district might identify remodeling needs or student transportation as most important. Scientific surveys can test multiple options to see which investments will result in increased support by those registered voters most likely to cast ballots.

COST

Whether it is a major investment in new construction or in lower primary class sizes, putting the right "what" on the ballot is only half the battle. When asked in postelection surveys why an election failed in their community, "cost was too high" is one of the two most frequently cited explanations by voters. Therefore, determining the community's appetite for spending is the second key dimension to consider when crafting the ballot question. Paraphrasing from a study of New York elections, "Each district has its own collective demand for education under varying tax cost conditions" (Sclafani, 1985, p. 25). Therefore, scientific surveys need to test local taxpayers' willingness to part with their hard-earned money to improve their public schools.

Effective surveys test voters' reactions under different taxing conditions, measuring support not only below but also somewhat above what the school district deems necessary to address facility or program needs. As the line measuring support intersects with the 50th percentile,[1] the survey clearly reveals at what tax impact the district will fail to achieve a "yes" voting majority. With that in mind, wise districts back off from this maximum acceptable tax rate far enough not only to factor in the survey instrument's error of measurement but also to provide for an additional margin for victory.

STRUCTURE

Splitting the ballot can be an effective strategy, particularly in cases in which the tax tolerance is low, when the community has a history of organized opposition, or when survey results suggest that voters are demanding more choice. Although still unusual, some school districts are responding to this unbundling strategy in a big way—particularly after one or more losses—by serving voters a smorgasbord of five or more ballot questions that are either contingent or freestanding. In some cases, splitting the ballot in this manner can serve to divide the "no" vote and thus lessen the likelihood and intensity of organized opposition by providing smaller bites and greater choice.

Regardless of election type, your school district shares one thing in common with all others—a stratified electorate ranging from "boosters" to "detractors." Somewhere in between is the largest block of persuadable voters, most of whom could be described as either "soft yes" or "soft no." Additionally, there are voters who will still have no opinion on the eve of the election campaign and who can best be described as the "undecideds." Behavior on either end of the spectrum is both predictable and uniform, with boosters voting consistently "yes" and detractors overwhelmingly "no." Ballot splitting may have minimal—but positive—effect on your most ardent boosters and detractors, but it can significantly alter voting patterns among the persuadable voters (see Figure 6.1). The goal of the two-part ballot is to split the "no" vote and leverage additional "yes" votes in support of the main question. This strategy can also impact the formation and intensity of opposition.

Organized opposition is the foe of special elections requiring taxpayer approval. Paraphrasing from the work of Philip Piele and John Hall, the grandfathers of school election research, school issues are uniquely susceptible to group-based attacks. Therefore, the more organized the opposition, the more likely the election will fall to defeat. Splitting the ballot can bring two new and powerful factors to the equation and influence the presence or absence of organized opposition, as well as the intensity of these groups. First, splitting the proposal ensures the school board can keep the cost of the main question within the community's appetite for spending as determined by the pre-election polling. Second, and consistent with Marketing 101, the individual price tags of two or more separate ballot questions will always seem less than the total cost of a single question carrying the full weight of the proposal. Staying within the community's collective comfort zone and lowering the "sticker shock" by using two ballot questions can ease concern about the election, discourage formation of organized opposition, and reduce the energy of a proposal's detractors.

A split ballot should be considered if one or more of the following criteria are present:

- The cost of a single ballot question exceeds the community's comfort level as determined by a pre-election survey.
- There is a history or likelihood of organized opposition.
- There is a logical way to divide the district's proposal between what is absolutely essential and what is important but of secondary priority.

Single Question Q1 $20 Million	Proposal	Split Ballot Q1 $14 Million Q2 $6 Million
100% "Yes" Votes	Boosters	100% "Yes" Votes
70% "Yes" Votes	Soft "Yes"	80% "Yes" Q1 60% "Yes" Q2
50% "Yes" Votes	Undecided	60% "Yes" Q1 40% "Yes" Q2
30% "Yes" Votes	Soft "No"	40% "Yes" Q1 20% "Yes" Q2
100% "No" Votes	Opponents	100% "No" Votes
50% "Yes" 50% "No" Toss-Up	Outcome	Q1 56% "Yes" 44% "No" Q2 44% "Yes" 56% "No"

Figure 6.1. Use of Ballot-Splitting to Alter Voting Patterns

- There is an opportunity or need to leverage more "yes" votes in support of the main question by activating a block of citizens willing to work for passage of the first proposal in order to have a chance at passing the second question.

Jumping on the split-ballot bandwagon is not the right strategy in all situations and will not guarantee victory. Sometimes splitting a proposal is simply not feasible. One cannot propose to fund half of the new middle school in Question 1 and the other half in Question 2. In other situations, the strategy of splitting the ballot may result in confusion or unwanted controversy. School districts vary greatly, and every election is conducted within a unique and complex context. The "splitting" strategy should be considered when a district is expecting a close or highly contested election or when the cost of the whole package exceeds the community's comfort level. A carefully designed split ballot, aligned with a community's priorities and willingness to pay, could be the difference between winning and losing your next bond or operating election.

Splitting is not the only structural characteristic of the ballot question to consider. In some instances, districts might offer three or more questions on a single ballot or design a contingent relationship between two or more proposals. Districts must also deliberate the order of the ballot questions when two or more proposals are presented. Although we do not cite specific research on this point, successful practice strongly suggests that school districts should always lead with their top priority. Common sense would dictate that most voters will associate multiple ballot questions with an increasing and cumulative impact on their taxes as they move down the ballot. Ballot fatigue—resulting in fewer "yes" votes for later proposals as compared with the first question—must be considered. Everything else being equal, it is more likely the first proposal will pass than a second or third question.

In terms of the number of questions, how many are too many? Since there is no "magic number," school leaders must ensure there is a logical reason for multiple questions and that the rationale for doing so can be effectively explained to the community. Splitting the district's proposal into multiple questions—for the purpose of offering voters more choices—will not be an asset if it leads only to confusion and controversy. In addition to the number of questions, school districts also must decide if a secondary ballot question will be freestanding—to go up or down on its own merits—or contingent on the first proposal passing.

In states that allow contingent questions, a second or third ballot proposal can be designed to be contingent on the first question passing. The actual ballot language for a contingent question might begin by stating, "If Question 1 is approved by the electorate, do you also want to authorize. . . ." So, under what set of circumstances might it make sense to structure a continent ballot question? One example is in rapidly growing school districts in which construction bonds are needed to build additional school buildings. If the district cannot afford to absorb the increased operating expenses of a new school and enrollment growth does not generate enough new revenue, a district might request more operating money in Question 1 and then have a second contingent question seeking bonding authority to build the school. The intent of this ballot structure is to communicate to the voters that the district cannot afford to build a new building without the additional revenue to staff and run the school.

The same strategy can be used for an operating levy with Question 1, for example, seeking additional revenue to add more teachers to reduce class sizes, with a contingent Question 2 requesting more resources for gifted and talented or remedial programs. In this example, the split ballot structure with a contingent second question accomplishes two goals. First, the structure of the ballot clearly differentiates between the district's core mission and most urgent need and other important, but secondary, proposals. In essence, the district is telling the community, through the structure of the ballot questions, that if it cannot afford to put a sufficient number of teachers in the classroom, then it certainly is not going to invest in other programs. The second advantage of this ballot structure is that it allows for an exercise in community-based decision making that can help blunt the attack of those in opposition. By proposing a two-part ballot and asking for direct community involvement in setting the school district's priorities, it is much more difficult for opponents to haggle over minor details in any part of the proposal.

The best campaign in the world will not be successful if the content, cost, and structure of the ballot question miss the mark. School districts must use information from the scientific survey and count book to align their proposal with their community. A carefully developed ballot question provides advocates with what all salespeople seek: the right product at the right cost in the right package.

NOTE

Portions of this chapter were previously published in "Lessons from the Bond Battlefield," which appeared in the November 2001 *American School Board Journal*. Copyright 2001 National School Boards Association. All rights reserved.

1. For those states requiring more than a simple majority, the bar gets set a bit higher.

CHAPTER 7

Ongoing and Targeted Communications

"Every school, school district and organization has public relations—just like everyone has a personality."

National School Public Relations Association, 2002

Whether intentional and planned or random and unfocused, school districts communicate a variety of messages to the public *and* their employees every day of the week. Considering the importance and positive impact of an effective public relations program, a district should avoid the mistake of trying to design such a program in the midst of a demanding and complex school finance campaign.

Instead, school districts are wise to develop ongoing public relations processes in which all communication-related messages are part of a comprehensive communication system planned and coordinated at the district level. By establishing an ongoing communication framework, a district in the throes of a bond election campaign can focus primarily on the need to alter the *content* of communications, as compared with its volume or delivery methods.

So how would a district know if its communication program is comprehensive and ongoing? According to the National School Public Relations Association (NSPRA), an exemplary communication system incorporates seven key components:

1. The approval of the superintendent/CEO
2. A focus on meeting the goals of the organization and ultimately improving education and, to the extent possible, enhancing student achievement

> **PUBLIC ENGAGEMENT**
>
> The concept of public engagement, unlike the common understanding of public relations or communications, is a "two-way process involving both internal and external publics with the goal of stimulating better understanding of the role, objectives, accomplishments, and needs of the organization" (National School Public Relations Association, 2002). In school districts where public engagement is a core value, community members as well as staff are seen as partners. Ongoing communications is something done *with* the public not *to* the public and is focused on a broad set of goals. In this context, passing a school finance election becomes a subset of this ongoing system, not its sole purpose.

3. Identification of target audiences and the use of research data to identify key messages and strategies for delivering those messages
4. Communication plans for specific program changes or initiatives developed in conjunction with the staff responsible for them
5. Identification of who will be affected and the strategies for reaching them
6. To the extent possible, use of measurable goals for behavior change or accomplishment, deadlines, responsibilities, resources, and strategies
7. Regular review to ensure communication efforts remain relevant, are on schedule, and are adjusted whenever necessary to reach planned goals or to deal with emerging needs and opportunities (NSPRA, 2002)

The first step in communication planning—long before any talk of budgets, bonds, or ballots—is to audit your district's public relations program against these seven criteria. Development of an effective and ongoing public relations program is the foundation for communication planning during your finance election.

COMMUNICATION STRATEGIES FOR SCHOOL FINANCE ELECTIONS

Barbara Nicol Public Relations identifies four key steps (also known as RPCE) for school finance election planning within the context of a comprehensive communication system:

- Research
- Plan
- Communicate
- Evaluate

The *research* step starts with careful examination of data from the postelection analysis, the count book, and the community survey. These complementary planning tools hold the keys to answering three questions vital to communication planning:

- Which voters are most likely to cast ballots in the upcoming election?
- What is the head count of key blocs of voters as a proportion of all registered voters?
- How do key blocs of voters perceive components of the school district's proposal?

Strategic use of the three data components help the communication team develop core and subordinate messages that align with the values of the registered voters most likely to cast election day ballots. For example, examination of the postelection analysis might reveal that residents age 55 and older cast ballots in disproportionately high numbers in odd-year elections. If the election you are planning is during an odd-numbered year, the count book can yield information as to how many of these older voters reside in the district, as well as their gender, address, phone number, and likelihood to vote. The strategic approach to this bloc of citizens will vary depending upon, for example, if they represent 10% of the registered voters in the district or 30%. Last, and most important for communication planning, is to determine

> **CORE MESSAGE AND SUBORDINATE MESSAGE**
>
> According to Barb Nicol, president of Barbara Nicol Public Relations, a district's core message should be the one thing the district wants the voters to remember when they cast their ballots. Following are examples of a core and subordinate message for a bond election:
>
> - **Core message:** "A new middle school is vitally important to our students, staff, and the future of this community. Our students deserve to be educated in a school that is safe, up-to-date, and spacious enough to meet the needs of the growing student body."
> - **Subordinate message** (targeted to older voters): "Eighty years ago our parents and grandparents built a school for us. The old school has served us well, but now it's time to reinvest—our turn to give back—to make sure that our children and grandchildren can reach their full potential in a safe and modern school."

how this 55-and-older group views the main components of the district's proposal.

A well-designed survey bolsters the research step by determining *where* most residents get their information about the local public schools. When asked the question, "What information source do you primarily rely upon for information about the school district?" responses will range from a local newspaper to a child's teacher to word of mouth. Each community is different in how it responds to this question, which has significant implications for how the school district and campaign deliver their messages to the voters.

Data from the postelection analysis, count book, and survey allow the district not only to emphasize the right core themes, but also to target specific messages to discrete audiences. Relative to our example of 55-and-older voters, a district would want to focus on how older adults would like to see their tax dollars spent. Careful examination of these data provides the district with a road map for the second step in the process—communication planning.

Establishing a *plan* for a school finance election involves applying the information gleaned during the research step and translating it into a master communication plan for the school district and campaign committee. The school district's communication plan—limited to information rather than advocacy in most states—is best developed by answering four questions:

- What is proposed?
- How much will it cost me?
- Why should I vote for it?
- What happens if it passes or fails?

The answers to these questions form the basis for public meetings and informational material provided by the school district.

Although informational rather than persuasive, school district communications should be coordinated with campaign committee communications by focusing on the same core messages and emphasizing the benefits to students. In turn, the campaign committee's planning also begins by answering the same four questions posed above with a constant eye on the community survey's findings. The campaign's mission extends beyond information to advocacy; therefore, core messages focused on students are delivered with greater intensity and emotional punch. These messages are communicated many times and in many ways to all audiences. In support of these overriding messages, planning also includes development of a set of complementary, subordinate messages for specific audiences.

The third step in the process is the delivery of core and subordinate messages to targeted audiences during the *communication* phase of the process. An important characteristic of outstanding work in this key step involves repetition of core messages in a variety of formats. In addition to the commonplace, campaigns have been known to use everything from windsocks to fortune cookies to get their core messages across to the voters. Remember that for some voters it will be the eighth iteration of the key message that finally flips the light switch. Excellence in this communication phase also maximizes use of data to differentiate messages to targeted audiences.

And do not forget to monitor the communication plan to balance the competing objectives of sticking to the core message while maintaining a degree of flexibility for reacting to unforeseen circumstances. In implementing the communication phase, school districts are urged to add the following three strategies to their communications tool box:

- The message sandwich
- The 80/20 rule
- The 3 Cs of communication: clear, concise, and compelling

The last key step in a well-designed communication plan is to *evaluate*. Win or lose, it is important to debrief staff, key volunteers, and other community members. How did people react to the district's informational brochure or the campaign's persuasive fact sheet, which was intended to present essential information about the district's proposal? How well did the core messages from the campaign committee complement the informational material from the school district? Did feedback from public meetings, letters to the editor, and other forums demonstrate that the public understood the content and rationale for the district's proposal? This information can be obtained in a variety of ways including in-depth interviews, focus groups, surveys, and soliciting feedback from other communication professionals in a jury of peers. Answering such questions represents the first step toward building a foundation for success in your next bond or operating levy.

If you expect to run a school finance election in the future, the time to start building your public relations program is now. Often fewer than 30% of registered voter households contain children enrolled in the local public schools—certainly not enough voters to win most tax campaigns. This demographic reality makes it all the more important for school district and campaign leaders to execute the RPCE steps within the context of a broader public engagement plan. Public relations that is grounded in engagement with the public, focused on clear goals, *and* ongoing throughout the year will provide a solid foundation and substantially improve your chances on election day.

TARGETED FLIERS

The campaign fliers in Figures 7.1, 7.2, and 7.3 are from a school district seeking support to build a new middle school as well as raising additional property taxes. This single-sheet flier, mailed by the campaign committee, illustrates use of both core and subordinate messages, as well targeting messages to specific audiences. The first page emphasizes the two core messages about the district's proposal to build a new middle school and raise more operating money for programs. Core messages such as these go to all voters and are repeated multiple times and in a variety of formats. The second and third examples depict two different versions of the back of this single-sheet flyer. One is designed for parents of preschool students and the other for public school parents and senior citizens. Through the use of integrated databases—the same database used for the post-voter analysis, count book, and survey—the campaign committee can draw appropriate mailing labels to deliver the most salient messages to the right audiences.

It's time to reinvest...
in our children, our schools, our community.

On September 10, we face a critical decision.

Do we reinvest in our children and our community, or do we turn our backs on our future? Area Schools need our support.

Join your friends and neighbors to Vote YES YES – approval of both questions will cost less than $14/month for the owner of a $150,000 home! Communities with good schools are more vital, their property values are stronger, they attract good businesses and they are good places to live. It's time to reinvest.

☒ **YES**   ☒ **YES**

Vote YES for a Revenue Increase

Our schools need more money to meet our kids' learning needs. The state limits how much money schools receive – but we can vote to give them more. Because school funding is not keeping pace with escalating heating, insurance and educational costs, the district will have to increase class sizes and reduce programs if this referendum question doesn't pass. It simply costs more to provide up-to-date technology, quality programs and healthy learning environments. Our kids can't afford more budget cuts. **We need to reinvest... in our children, our schools and our community.**

Vote YES for a New Middle School

We can no longer afford to maintain the 79-year-old middle school, much less repair it. It leaks, it has fungus and the sewage backs up. Our middle schoolers need a healthy learning environment, up-to-date facilities and classrooms that support efficient, project-based learning. A new middle school makes good financial and educational sense. It will attract the best teachers and will save millions of dollars over other options. Building a new middle school is a top priority of the district's long-range plans and will benefit our community. **We need to reinvest in a new middle school.**

to reinvest in our kids

Your time and contributions are needed to support this campaign for our kids. Please help.

Figure 7.1.   Targeted Flier Examples. Designed by Barbara Nicol Public Relations

"Education is the key to my son's future. I'm doing everything I can to make sure Troy has good schools to attend — like Vote Yes Yes on September 10!"

Area Schools need more money and a new middle school. It's up to our community to support our schools. Listen to your friends and neighbors and Vote Yes Yes to Reinvest on September 10.

Figure 7.2. Targeted Flier Examples. Designed by Barbara Nicol Public Relations

"From an employer's perspective it's critical to invest in one of our most prized assets, the youth we're teaching in our schools. That's why I'm voting YES YES on September 10."

"A new middle school has been planned since before I went there in 1977, and current school district funding isn't keeping up with rising costs. Our kids can't afford any more budget cuts — we need to pass both school referendum questions on September 10!"

"Someone provided an education for me, someone built those schools, someone paid for them, and now we have the responsibility to do that for the next generations. It's time to reinvest — I'm voting YES YES September 10 and I hope you will, too."

Area Schools need more money and a new middle school.

It's up to our community to support our schools.

Listen to your friends and neighbors and Vote YES YES to Reinvest September 10.

Figure 7.3. Targeted Flier Examples. Designed by Barbara Nicol Public Relations

MESSAGE SANDWICH

The message sandwich strategy, developed by Jeff Ansell, president of Jeff Ansell & Associates, not only helps to articulate and refine core and subordinate messages but also provides a handy tool for those individuals caught in the glare of the television camera. Like a well-constructed sandwich, there are top and bottom slices to hold things together and lots of good stuff in between to provide substance, flavor, and texture.

The Top Slice

"The top priority of this school district is constructing a new middle school. The current building is more than 80 years old, unsafe, and can no longer meet the needs of our students and programs. New construction makes more sense and avoids excessive tax money wasted on repairs."

Between the Slices

- The current building has serious structural, safety, and classroom deficiencies.
- It is more cost-effective over time to construct a new school rather than pour more money into repairing the old building.
- We are losing dozens of families and tens of thousands of dollars every year to neighboring schools with better middle school facilities.
- The new school will offer a modern library, up-to-date science and computer labs, and adequate space for a growing student body.
- The new school will provide students and staff with a safe environment absent of concerns about asbestos, mold, and poor ventilation.

The Bottom Slice

"A new middle school is a good investment and vitally important to our students, our staff, and the future of this community. Our students deserve to be educated in a school that is safe, up-to-date, and spacious enough to meet the needs of the growing student body."

THE 80/20 RULE

The 80/20 rule dictates "staying on message" while employing a stealthy block-and-parry technique with your toughest critics. To avoid your public meeting morphing into two hours of complaining about maintenance problems at the high school, use the 80/20 rule to get back on message. When questions or critics take the focus off message:

- Respectively acknowledge
- Briefly respond
- Return to your message

At the end of the meeting, the goal should be that at least 80% of the talk time was focused on your message.

Question at Public Meeting

"You guys keep talking about building a new middle school instead of what really needs to be done. The high school is a maintenance mess and a hazard to students. I say build a new high school instead along with some remodeling at the middle school. The high school is my main priority and that's where the money should go. We do not need a new middle school."

Responding Using the 80/20 Rule

"Thanks for your comment. You bring up a good point. The facility task force, made up of citizens just like you, has identified eight priority maintenance projects at the high school, all of which need to be done and all of which will be done if this bond election passes. The most pressing need, however, is a new middle school. The old building turned 80 this month, is too small for a growing student body, does not meet state fire and safety codes, and does not support the needs of students who wish to achieve a first-rate education. A new middle school is our first priority and must be replaced. We can build a new middle school and improve the high school with one-third less cost to our taxpayers."

THE 3 Cs OF COMMUNICATION

Communication produced by school districts and campaign committees is notoriously lacking the 3 Cs—clear, concise, and compelling. Across all types of school districts, citizens routinely blame cost and poor communications as the reasons finance elections failed in their community. Their collective fingers of blame—pointed by taxpayers at their school districts—often complain of jargon, legalese, and "educationese" as barriers to both understanding and support. To be fair, state laws often limit a school board's discretion in designing optimal ballot language and require specific language that is often obtuse. There is much room, however, for improved clarity in communications that are fully within the control of school districts and campaign committees.

Unclear

"The media center will be expanded to provide for a large, multipurpose room for students' end-of-quarter capstone presentations or for teams of teachers to use for interdisciplinary classes."

Clear

"The library will be expanded to provide teachers with a larger classroom to use for special projects, for student speeches and presentations, or when two or more classes are working together on an assignment."

The technique of split sampling (i.e., half of the respondents are given a different version of the same question) in community surveys is another way to test the clarity of your language. In an Iowa survey, half of the registered voters were asked if they would pay more in taxes to upgrade the school media centers. The other half was asked if they would support a tax hike to modernize the school libraries. In this survey, there was more support for upgrading the libraries. Paraphrasing a former Minnesota governor, it is not clear unless it can pass the barbershop test.

Also of considerable challenge is striking the right balance on the concise versus verbose continuum. More is not better if "more" means page after page of narrative, charts, and long-winded letters from the superintendent or school board president. Rather, experienced public-relations experts encourage clear and concise messages, with appropriate supporting data repeated frequently in varying formats. Concise communications happen when "more" relates to the frequency of messages, not their individual length.

The last of the 3 Cs—compelling—exhorts school district and campaign communicators to use the richness of our language, graphics, and photographs to generate some passion and imagery to help persuade voters to support a proposal and remember the campaign's key messages. Given the limitations on what school districts can do relative to advocating the proposal, addressing the compelling standard is mostly left in the hands and imaginations of the campaign committee. Drawing insight from the community survey and their own experiences, seasoned communication experts can effectively impact voters' attitudes with compelling messages and designs. One of the best examples of a compelling theme is that of a turtle, depicted in Figure 7.4 in a postcard campaign piece. The turtle symbolizes a core message that this suburban district is "dead last" in terms of class size. The image of the turtle was a powerful centerpiece of this successful campaign.

Figure 7.4. Turtle Theme. Designed by Agenzia LLC

CHAPTER 8

Planning

If you skipped to this chapter to copy down our suggested campaign plan, turn back to the beginning of the book and start reading. Every part of this book is designed to help you plan and execute a successful campaign in your school district. It does not, however, contain a copy of "The Doctors' Patented Winning Campaign Plan." The reason is simple: No single plan exists that can meet the needs of every school district and every election environment. But there is a process that will allow you to create one for your district.

The process of writing a complete campaign plan will be one of the most overwhelming tasks a school leader will ever undertake. Even when a district brings in professional consulting to help guide it through the process of planning and executing a school finance campaign, the process is one that demands all of the time, energy, and talent school leaders have to offer. Preparing for, planning, and executing a campaign must, if done properly, distract the superintendent, the school board, key staff, and the parents from the tasks they perform during a normal school year. The process of successfully planning and executing a campaign actually has a great deal in common with an annual event with which most of us have a great deal of experience. If you routinely plan and cook Thanksgiving dinner so that everything arrives on the table hot, well prepared, handsomely presented, and cooked to perfection while the guests take their seats just as the last of the serving dishes are placed on the table, you have an understanding of the skills it takes to plan and execute a school finance campaign. And, just as you spent time learning the techniques of preparing this annual family feast from parents and relatives, you need to take time now to learn an approach to campaign planning that will give you the necessary tools to create an effective, winning campaign plan.

BASIC RULES

Before beginning a discussion of our approach to planning, however, there are some basic rules that apply to all school finance campaigns. These rules will apply throughout the planning process. Although following all of them will not guarantee you a victory, ignoring them can ensure a loss.

- *Start planning early.* If you are reading this book in January and know your district will place a proposal on the November ballot, do not put the book down and figure you will start applying what you have learned closer to election day. Given all that must be done to fully prepare a school district for a school finance campaign, January is awfully close—maybe too close—to November. In most cases, give yourself at least 12 months. And remember the summer is a very difficult time to get anything done. Never assume you will get half of what you planned to do on the campaign done between June and September.
- *Make sure that any plan that is produced coordinates the activities of the school district and the citizens' campaign that will form to support the proposal.* The laws of each state place various restrictions on district activities. But throughout the planning process, you are creating one campaign in which the district and citizens will have clearly defined roles. Every activity is coordinated.
- *Review all district policies that may impact the ability of your campaign to develop.* These may include data privacy policies or the manner in which parent e-mail addresses are collected.
- *Find and use outside talent where it will expand the expertise found in your district office and school buildings.* A school finance election will require the school district to use skills and talents that are not a part of its regular operations. No district's budget is unlimited, but long experience has taught us that a school finance election is

not the time or place to be penny wise and pound-foolish. A district is wise to start early in assembling the team that will help it plan and execute a victory at the ballot box.

BUILDING YOUR TEAM

- *Make sure you have the legal and financial help you need.* Even though the district has lawyers and financial planners who help with day-to-day operations, the district will need to consult lawyers and financial advisors who specialize in school finance proposals. Lawyers who specialize in school finance proposals will quickly provide you with the legal deadlines with which you must comply and an outline of the legal documents that must be prepared before you can go onto the ballot. Financial advisors can provide you with accurate estimates of the cost to the average voter in the district of the proposal you want to place on the ballot.
- *Consult with outside architects and engineers.* In many districts, the facilities department is quite capable of describing and documenting the challenges facing the districts' classrooms and buildings. It is important to have this work checked and rechecked, however, by outside architects and engineers familiar with the questions voters will ask the district once a proposal is placed on the ballot.
- *Realize curriculum review is an ongoing process.* Preparation for a campaign may require the district to bring in outside facilitators to expand the normal review process to include an attempt to quantify and make specific the district's vision of the classroom education it wants to provide in the future.
- *Hire communications and community research specialists.* Although the district may have excellent communications and assessment departments, there are communications and community research specialists who work almost exclusively with school finance proposals. Do not hesitate to learn from them how survey research and communications planning differs when the goal is a "yes" vote on a local proposal.
- *Seek out campaign consultants who can assist in the process of turning your desire to address a financial challenge or improve your schools into a concrete plan for winning on election day.* Such a consultant should never replace the army of school people you will need to win, but his or her understanding of how to structure a campaign can save you the time you might otherwise spend "reinventing the wheel."
- *If a campaign plan is not written down, it does not exist.*

PLANNING

Now let's look at a framework for examining your district's specific situation and creating a campaign plan that will meet your specific needs. If your district has never been on the ballot, it will help you think through all of the steps involved in creating an effective, winning plan for your first campaign. If you have campaigned before and lost, it should help you look at your district, its needs, and your community in a different way. In *Reframing Organizations,* Bolman and Deal (1991) introduce four "lenses" or "frames" for organizational analysis:

- Structural
- Human resource
- Political
- Symbolic

Viewing your situation through these lenses and approaching the next election with this framework in mind can help you engage in the process of winning with an integrated, comprehensive plan.

THE STRUCTURAL FRAME

The structural frame relates to coordinating, organizing, controlling, planning, goal setting, and clarifying expectations. From this, strategies develop. If you have never been on the ballot before, use all the data available in an annotated voter file and in demographic district maps to understand *who* the voters in your district are. There will be key questions to answer. Are district parents registered to vote? If they are registered, do they participate or does it take a presidential election to get most of them to the polls? Does the ethnic background of your student and parent population match that of the population of registered voters? Very often, district leadership is surprised to find that although more than half of their students are from minority populations, minorities still make up a small percentage of the voting population in the district. If your district has been on the ballot sometime during the last few years, expand your knowledge of the voters in the district by completing a postelection analysis. Learn everything possible about your district through the statistics that define it and its voting population.

Expand what you have learned by using survey research where appropriate to explore the degree to which the community around you understands the challenges facing the district and shares your goals for the future. These research tools will allow you to develop a clear understanding of the community's core values. You can then work to present the community with a school finance proposal that is well-aligned with their expectations.

Fully evaluate all district communications by asking someone from outside the district to review the materials you have been producing. Work with your state's public relations association or a private consultant to understand which parts of your current communications program are working and, most important, which are not. During this process, it is very important to find those places in your communications where you are speaking in the jargon of an educator. Though such language is extremely useful as you communicate with colleagues and peers, it may not communicate your challenges, goals, and solutions effectively to the large number of noneducators who will be asked to vote for your proposal.[1]

Finally, as you learn more and more about your district, use this material to write a detailed and comprehensive plan. Capture details about the challenges you face. If you cannot quantify the ways in which additional tax funds will be spent, add to your timeline the steps needed to complete a facility's audit or curriculum review. After an evaluation of district communications, outline the steps that will be required to improve the program's effectiveness. Following the creation of an annotated voter file and, possibly, postelection analysis, determine whether parents within the district are registered and whether they vote. If they are not voters, make sure the plan includes ways to increase parental registration and participation. If there are areas of the district that may oppose—or always have opposed—school taxes, make sure the plan captures your best thoughts and ideas about how you will overcome these potential "no" votes. When the plan is finished, move on to recruit capable people to execute it.

THE HUMAN RESOURCE FRAME

The human resource frame relates to involving people through an understanding of each individual's feelings, needs, preferences, abilities, and desire for participation. Begin with an honest evaluation of the leadership being provided by the school board, superintendent, administrators, teachers, staff, and parent volunteers. Evaluate that leadership as it applies to the events of the current school year and then look into the district's past. Base the evaluation of the leadership available in the district on qualitative and quantitative data. A realistic assessment of the leadership resources available in your district will have a direct impact on the success of the campaign and the district's ability to meet the need of students through the ballot proposal.

Just as there are professionals who can help you review district communications, there are professionals who specialize in helping school districts plan and execute school finance campaigns. Do not hesitate to bring these consultants into the district to assist in the evaluation of your leadership resources. Because they have gone through the process of planning and executing school finance campaigns more times than any superintendent ever should, they can offer valuable insight into the human resources available in your district. They also can provide invaluable support as you work to motivate your election team and win your campaign.

Finally, as you work to identify and solicit leadership for your campaign use the *ideal task performer* philosophy. No matter what job needs to be done, there is an ideal task performer to do it. Think for a moment about two jobs that almost every campaign has: someone who coordinates the activities of the campaign volunteers and someone who actively recruits those volunteers. If two people have expressed an interest in these jobs, the campaign will most likely be best served if the detail-oriented introvert takes on the role of coordinator while the extroverted chair of the PTA takes on the job of recruiting people to work in the campaign. The more critical the task, the more important it is to find ideal task performers.

As you read, pay special attention to the verbs that were just used. Leadership will be identified, solicited, and recruited. This process involves work and time, all of which must be accounted for in your campaign plan. Many campaigns end the night the superintendent or school board president calls a meeting in the gym to ask if anyone would like to chair the district's upcoming school finance campaign. The approach we are recommending strongly suggests that developing a leadership team is both strategic and "hands on" and discards the notion that the superintendent would call a meeting in the school cafeteria to find volunteers to chair the campaign. Identifying, soliciting, and finding the leadership needed for a campaign is a process. Provide time for it in your campaign plan and define the specific steps you will need to take to complete it. Finally, remember that all leaders, whether staff, parent volunteers, or community members, must also be chosen with a keen sense of how they will be perceived by the public.

In addition to leaders, every campaign needs volunteers. The best campaigns apply Tom Sawyer's philosophy and involve a lot of people. If 5 volunteers might complete the job of canvassing a neighborhood near the district office, recruit 10. For every job where it makes sense, involve as many people as possible. Their involvement will make light work of many of the campaign's most difficult or mundane tasks. In addition, the more that teachers, staff, and parents invest in the campaign—both through the hours they volunteer and the dollars they donate—the more likely they are to remember to end the campaign by casting a ballot. As you develop a campaign plan, quantify your need for volunteer hours and list the ways in which volunteers will be recruited.

DIFFICULT AND MUNDANE?

Not all the tasks that must be completed to win a campaign are exciting. A sign used to hang in the Government Relations office of one of the nation's largest teacher organizations. It read: "Campaigns take the brightest, most energetic people in your organization and ask them to complete the most boring, mundane tasks you can imagine."

THE POLITICAL FRAME

The political frame focuses on the conflict, negotiations, influence, and interplay among different constituencies, interest groups, and organizations. This frame will include how you approach the leaders of the political parties in your community and how you plan to make contact with those groups of voters that your post-election analysis, demographic mapping, or community survey tell you are most likely to resist your effort to raise taxes. Begin with the positive by identifying community VIPs and solicit their opinions and support. Seek out "blockbuster" endorsements, especially from individuals who "everyone" might assume will oppose your school finance proposal. If you have been on the ballot and lost, this will include looking for converts who will change from a public "no" to a public "yes."

Often as a school leader, you are not in a position to directly influence the members of the community most likely to oppose you. But that does not mean that you cannot reach out and ask for the help of supporters who can influence those groups or individuals. Two examples will illustrate. A district that lost two school finance elections knew that its proposal failed due to an antitax vote in the community. No argument the school community made concerning the need for classroom programs and well-maintained buildings influenced the leaders of these antitax voters. Before its next election, the district solicited and received the support of members of the business community. With their help, they built a strong case for the school tax around the idea that local property values were being threatened by a weakened school district. This argument, presented with the help of the local business community, was able to influence some of the antitax voters, thus reducing the number of "no" votes cast to the point that the district passed its proposal.

The second example involved some background research. A school district lost a major school finance election because of the outspoken opposition of the local taxpayers association. After the loss, district leadership brought in the help it needed to assess the funding sources that were supporting the taxpayers groups. Once identified, the district was able to talk with supporters who worked for many of the companies that were supplying the taxpayers with campaign funds. Those employees were able to slow down and in some cases stop the flow of funding to the taxpayers after they talked to their bosses and coworkers about what the loss meant to classroom programs throughout the district. As you develop a campaign plan, think about ways that you can convert or isolate potential opponents. Quantify the steps involved and provide ample time in your campaign calendar.

The political framework also demands that you be very clear about how a loss (or a previous defeat) impacts the community and its children. All school finance campaigns live with some built-in limitations. You cannot build your campaign on the threat that a loss will mean that you will shut down the entire third grade. School leaders, principals, and teachers will do everything in their power to keep schools and classrooms open regardless of how much funding the legislature or the community takes away. But as it approaches a campaign, district leadership must be willing to state very clearly the consequences of winning or losing on election day. Thinking through those consequences and writing them down is an essential part of planning. You must identify what is at risk and you must be willing to tell people that their vote will make a difference. You cannot exaggerate because school will be open on the day after the election and the community will see what happens. People will not vote "yes," however, if doing so *might* or *could* or *probably* or *maybe* will cause something to happen. Be clear and firm.

Finally, explore opportunities to create cognitive dissonance and remove anger in the community. For the purpose of this discussion, the influence of cognitive dissonance creates an internal struggle within the voter between their historical tendency to vote "no" and an emerging attitude of support. The dictionary definition of *dissonance* is "discord." In music, dissonance is a combination of tones that are not harmonious and suggest an unrelieved tension. Cognitive dissonance is a thought process that attempts to reconcile an internal conflict or paradox in one's mind. In finance elections, cognitive dissonance is created when conflict and uncertainty exist within individuals or groups that might typically be expected to oppose the election. For example, retired voters living on fixed incomes will be conservative and over-represented among "no" voters. Inviting senior citizens to volunteer and participate in the schools will not only create a bridge to seniors, but will create cognitive dissonance.

Likewise, asking retirees who are supportive of the district's proposal to present it to other groups of older voters will have a much more meaningful impact than a presentation by the campaign chairs—both of whom may be 20 to 30 years younger than anyone in the audience. Finally, asking the assistance of service groups such as the American Legion to help with Flag Day observances not only connects them to children but also creates questions about the consequences of voting against educational funding. Cognitive dissonance may not change a "no" vote to a "yes" vote, but it will give reason to question the opposition and de-energize detractors who, rather than voting "no," may choose not to vote at all.

THE SYMBOLIC FRAME

The symbolic lens provides a view of the "meaning" of the campaign and presents standards for the participants to rally around. The symbolic presentation of the core issues in the campaign is important whether you plan to try to "fly below the radar" or to take your campaign down the middle of Main Street with drums beating and flags flying. How you translate the need for your school finance proposal into a statement that conveys both meaning and emotion is extremely important.

Since the only thing that will win a "yes" vote from the average voter is information about the need for the school finance proposal, all campaigns produce large quantities of written material. A two-page fact sheet may accompany a short letter outlining the need for the school finance proposal. Voters still needing more information will be offered a page of frequently asked questions or invited to visit the campaign's website on which every possible piece of persuasive information has been accumulated. But as these materials are created, they must convey more than the words they contain. At every opportunity, the words must be delivered in a package that will visually rally the reader to the district's cause. The choice of colors and photographs as well as the careful, artistic manner in which materials are laid out and typeset and even the paper selected for printing can help to emphasize the need for the school finance proposal.

One example will illustrate: A district developed a very detailed, written fact sheet that it planned to distribute to all voters in the community. Using an annotated voter file, it was able to divide the voter file into three parts: parents, voters who were 65 or older, and nonparent voters younger than 65. Using exactly the same text, it created three versions—each designed for use with a specific audience. The version of the fact sheet sent to parents used photographs of parents interacting with classroom teachers and young children to emphasize the content of the piece. The fact sheet sent to older voters used pictures of grandparents volunteering in the classroom and reading to young children. For the younger nonparent audience, a photograph depicting a young couple interacting with their neighbors and their neighbors' children accompanies the fact sheet. In the background, a strategically placed for sale sign adorns a lawn across the street. The visual materials added to each version of the fact sheet helped reinforce its message with its specific audience. Therefore, campaign planning will require that you not only outline the prose you need to write to present the school finance proposal to the community—it will require you to think of the ways in which that prose will be presented.

In addition, you will need to think through the "theater" associated with media contact during your campaign. A dry presentation of enrollment statistics and projections may convince the press your schools are overcrowded, but creatively placing a news reporter in an overcrowded portable classroom for a day may help to emphasize the point. However, photo opportunities should never be staged for the media. Someone will find out you packed 53 students into one classroom only for the hour the reporter could visit. However, when you provide information to the media, remember to do so with a symbolic framework that emphasizes the rightness of your campaign.

Two examples will help illustrate. After a very painful series of public meetings to cut the budget, a district was finally ready for the school board meeting during which a multimillion-dollar budget cut would be approved. Because the earlier meetings were exhausting and the subject was painful, no one from the district or board thought to ask any parents or teachers to attend the meeting. When the final vote came, the only person to speak was a retiree who thought more cuts ought to be made in the administration. As a result, instead of covering the cuts themselves, the media focused on the fact that more might have been done. This district forgot to surround its very difficult vote with an appropriate touch of theater. The delivery of the district's message would have improved if even a handful of parents had been present to state that these difficult cuts were going to have a serious impact on the students, district, and the community.

The second example concerns the selection of appropriate theater. A district that seriously needed to build more classrooms staged a press conference at the school they thought best for an outdoor news event.

It had a large bus turnaround, an ample front lawn, good short-term parking on the streets in front of the school for the media, and a good view of the growing number of portable classrooms being packed onto the school's athletic fields. Unfortunately, it was also a middle school. As the campaign chairs diligently presented the reasons a school bond was needed, the media became more fascinated with the antics of the middle-school students assembled behind the speakers. Good actors know they never want to be upstaged by a child, a dog, or, in this case, a group of middle-school students.

The process of evaluating the symbolic presentation of the campaign becomes increasingly important *if* a school finance campaign chooses to become more generally visible. The more visible a campaign becomes, the more the symbols of the campaign must become compelling and clearly build support for the proposal.

Before continuing, however, a digression. The word *if* was carefully chosen in the last paragraph. Buttons, signs, and banners all have a place in school finance campaigns. Each should be evaluated as part of the symbolic presentation of the campaign to the community. Often circumstances will dictate a campaign abandon any hope of "flying beneath the radar" and incorporate these more visible campaign tools. Two rules, however, should govern the use of such materials:

- *Can the campaign afford them?* If the campaign decides to use its available communications funds to buy buttons instead of printing its fact sheet, the campaign is headed in the wrong direction. People must have information and, therefore, unless you have very large buttons available, campaign dollars must be used for fact sheets long before they are used for buttons.
- *Will they provide the school finance campaign with a distinct advantage over those inclined to vote "no" or are you doing this because "every campaign" does?* If a district knows that it will be faced with a very visible opposition campaign, then going public in a big way has some distinct advantages. A massive display of buttons and signs can give the undecided a reason to vote "yes" and, if you are lucky, "no" voters a reason to switch as they see the breadth of support for the schools and community. If, however, there will be no visible opposition, a massive display of signs and

banners may only serve to remind the "no" voters to cast their ballots on election day. Every action the campaign takes needs to be evaluated to ensure it is clearly an action advantageous to the process of winning "yes" votes.

These four frameworks provide you with a way to begin to evaluate and quantify the specific challenges, resources, and strengths your district brings to a campaign. Writing the plan (remember, *writing* is the key word here) will demand that all of your thoughts and ideas be captured, evaluated, and defined in terms of volunteers needs, steps to completion, time required for each task, and impact of every activity under consideration. Campaigns should not attempt to complete every task they have ever seen used in another campaign. They need to identify those that will work in your district on the ballot you have selected for your school finance proposal. The end result will be detailed timelines and task descriptions that will take your district through months of preparation and approximately 10 weeks of active, public campaigning on your way to a win on election day.

NOTE

1. In reviewing all of the communications materials being produced by a district that delivered a very high-quality, child-centered education, they found the materials never used the words *child* or *children*. By making a conscious effort to use those words, they made their communication with the community much more effective.

CHAPTER 9

Leadership and Organization

Successful finance elections require strong leadership and effective organization. Using a military analogy, winning campaigns require a great battle plan; a professional, experienced general; precise execution by subordinates in the field; and strong logistical support. As generals morph to superintendents, however, the research is mixed in terms of how to best lead and organize a successful school finance campaign. Three constants apply to all school districts:

- The campaign must have strong leadership.
- The campaign must be well-organized.
- The campaign must identify and recruit the ideal task performers for each and every leadership function.

Within this context there are important roles for the superintendent, school board, staff, parent leaders, and volunteers that play out similarly in most school communities.

ROLE OF THE SCHOOL BOARD

The school board's critical role is one of the most often-tested variables in scholarly research and the most consistent in how it correlates with successful elections. Simply put, achieving and maintaining a unanimous, supportive, and engaged school board may be the campaign's most important asset. More than one researcher has warned against moving forward on a school finance election until this is achieved. The margins between winning and losing are just too slim to give wary taxpayers an excuse to vote "no" as a result of a split, schizophrenic, or vacillating school board that is unable to get its act together.

Although campaign laws vary as to the extent to which school board members may participate as advocates during a school finance election, it is generally a misconception that board members cannot or should not be supportive and engaged. In most states, individual board members—operating independently from their official duties—are free to volunteer their time and support to a campaign. The community's culture, survey results, and perception of school board members—individually and collectively—will dictate the optimal visibility of their roles. In conceptualizing the role of the school board, campaign planners should focus on the following key functions before and during the campaign:

- Maintaining focus on student needs
- Polling community opinions before final ballot decisions
- Providing unanimous resolution to conduct election
- Aligning final proposal with community values and its appetite for spending
- Involving citizens in the campaign
- Providing support to the administration and volunteer committee

ROLE OF THE SUPERINTENDENT

The superintendent's vital role is to either provide the needed leadership, planning, and expertise *or* to ensure that someone else does it effectively. As noted previously, university libraries are replete with research focused on the variables affecting the outcomes of school finance elections. Additionally, empirical data—capturing the latest strategies and techniques used by successful school districts—should be collected and analyzed. Similar to the role of any successful CEO, the superintendent must provide the leadership, direction, and strategic planning necessary to achieve the organization's priorities—in this case a successful bond or operating election. Equally important, once the course is set, someone must ensure the plan is executed at the highest level. Who provides this critical leadership—whether it's the superintendent or a designee—will vary depending on many factors including the size of the district and the viability of the current superintendent. Some of the key functions performed by the superintendent before and during the campaign include

- planning strategically and meticulously based on research and best practice.
- working closely with the advocacy campaign to execute, monitor, and coordinate efforts.
- knowing when to use experts to supplement local resources.
- obtaining support and participation from staff in cooperation with campaign committee.
- providing information, support, and resources to the campaign committee within parameters of state law.

ROLE OF FACULTY AND STAFF

Another mistake is to conclude that faculty and staff members cannot or should not be involved in advocacy roles in support of a school finance campaign. While school leaders certainly need to address this issue within the context of their state's election laws, faculty and staff generally are free to express and exercise their political rights. In fact, in most communities, visible and strong support from teachers, secretaries, custodians, and bus drivers will be an asset to the campaign. Conversely, the damage can be significant when large numbers of employees criticize the ballot proposal, how the school district has used money in the past, or the performance of the school board, superintendent, or staff. Equally troubling to the campaign are staff members who are unable to answer even basic questions posed by friends or neighbors. Although these problems are not fully under the school district's or campaign's control, they can be minimized by focusing on the needs of employees and investing in them in terms of providing information and responding to questions and concerns.

In the final analysis, those individuals ultimately responsible for campaign strategy and planning need to determine the optimal involvement of faculty and staff based on the culture within the community and how individuals and groups are generally perceived. Some of the key functions of faculty and staff before and during a school finance campaign include

- solidifying and strengthening relationships with primary constituency (i.e., parents).
- identifying ways to reach out and enhance secondary constituencies within the community.
- demonstrating good stewardship of what has already been provided.
- asking questions and staying informed.
- supporting and participating in the campaign.

ROLE OF CITIZENS' CAMPAIGN COMMITTEE

Unlike the responsibility of the school board, which is to inform all constituents of the school district's proposal, citizens involved in the campaign are driven by an advocacy mission focused on persuading as many residents as possible to cast "yes" votes on election day. The role of the campaign committee is fundamentally political in nature and, like any political campaign, should focus on making its case, identifying support, and motivating the right voters to get to the polls. Therefore, all registered voters should not be treated the same in terms of communications and get-out-the-vote strategies.

One of the biggest challenges—and often the Achilles' heal of unsuccessful campaigns—is a lack of consistency in message and poor coordination between the school district and campaign committee. For example, if the district can legally mail information to the community,[1] launching door-to-door or phone canvassing before the school district mails residents information does not build goodwill or better friendships within the school community. Such problems can be minimized or avoided by developing an integrated election plan that incorporates both school district and campaign tasks and timelines in one master-planning document. They can also be addressed by including the superintendent and school board chairperson on the campaign committee as exofficio participants. The remainder of the school board can serve in similar roles on the campaign's working committees. The citizens' campaign committee's key responsibilities include

- identifying an overall theme as well as core and subordinate messages.
- gaining influential support.
- strategically canvassing the community to identify probable "yes" voters.
- recruiting volunteers for leadership roles.
- implementing a campaign plan as directed by leadership.
- coordinating campaign activities with school district initiatives.

School boards, superintendents, staff, and leaders of the citizens' campaign committee almost always perform key roles in campaign planning and execution. This plays out very differently in various school communities, however, and must be evaluated based on local norms, the community's history and culture, and how well these players are perceived within the community. As this relates to the school districts in particular, one way to achieve the best alignment between individuals and groups is to test community perceptions in a pre-election survey before finalizing roles and responsibilities. Consider the following example of data that could be collected within the context of a broader community survey in preparation for a school finance election. (Note: In the following examples, numerical ratings represent positive to negative ratios.)

How would you rate the overall performance of the following individuals and groups within your local school district?

Key Players	District 1	District 2
Superintendent	5/1	3/4
School Board	5/1	1/1
Principals	3/1	3/2
Teachers	6/1	3/1

To what extent do you trust the credibility and information from the following individuals or groups?

Key Players	District 1	District 2
Superintendent	5/1	2/3
School Board	6/1	1/1
Principals	3/1	4/3
Teachers	8/1	2/1

In the District 1 sample, the superintendent's performance was rated positively (i.e., excellent or good) by five respondents for every one who rated it as fair or poor. Likewise, the superintendent had high trust levels in District 1. Note in District 2, however, that less than half of the respondents thought the superintendent was doing a good job with similarly poor marks on trust. In some communities (e.g., District 1), the superintendent can and should be the campaign's standard-bearer. In other districts (e.g., District 2), however, the superintendent would probably best serve the campaign in the background and let other leaders be in the spotlight. Carefully planned questions within the context of a broader community survey provide the campaign with a significant resource from which to link key leadership needs with ideal task performers. Collecting this kind of information before the election also creates a potential opportunity for the school board and superintendent to proactively work on those issues negatively affecting the public's perception.

Once the school district and campaign have coordinated election plans, are clear on roles and responsibilities, and understand the appropriate roles of key players, it is time to translate the requirements of the plan into an organizational framework and begin the process of recruiting individuals to fill critical leadership roles. Chapter 10 presents a prototype for an organizational structure, including a description of working committees and critical responsibilities. It is important to note that there is no right way to organize, and no particular structure will guarantee success. What is fundamentally important to any organizational paradigm, however, is the notion of an *ideal task performer* when it comes to filling leadership roles on the citizens' committee. For many campaigns, failing to do this is not only a missed opportunity, but also a fatal mistake.

Efforts to match the right people to the right job run the gambit from laissez faire to surgically precise. At the laissez faire end of the continuum, imagine a group of community members piling into the high school auditorium for the first planning meeting. As people find their chairs, someone stands, clears her throat, and says, "Who wants to be in charge of finances?" At the other end of the continuum, a small group of key leaders completes a task analysis of each leadership role and strategically assesses the essential requirements and skills of each leadership position. This approach is reinforced by a core value that the campaign's mission is far too important to settle for anyone but the best.

What is the profile of an ideal task performer? Seeking the following characteristics will aid in focusing your recruitment efforts:

- High level of credibility and respect
- Well known with a following or network
- Expertise and experience matched to the leadership role or task
- Interest in the task at hand
- Activist and doer
- Problem solver

Once your optimal "dream team" is identified on paper, you need to be equally strategic in how to get your prime recruit to "sign on the dotted line." One of the most effective techniques—adapted from social psychology—is to use triangulation (i.e., two individuals approaching the third person you want) when filling leadership positions. At one point of the triangle is a campaign volunteer who has already said "yes" to the committee's call to leadership. The second point of the triangle is the one person your prime recruit simply could not say "no" to when asked to serve. The third point of the triangle is the ideal task performer who is being recruited for a specific function on the committee. This common sense approach is consistent with our life experiences: It does make a difference who asks us for something, and it is more difficult to say "no" to two people versus one.

Bottom line? You are going for the "Wow!" factor when the community discovers who is actively working on the citizens' campaign committee. Once the leadership team is identified and trained, it is time to execute a winning campaign.

NOTE

1. The laws of each state differ concerning the degree to which school districts can distribute information once a proposal is placed on the ballot. As part of the planning process, make sure you understand all of the laws that might restrict district activity.

CHAPTER 10

Execution of Campaign

In Chapter 9, we spotlighted key roles of the school board, superintendent, faculty, and staff, as well as the citizens' campaign committee. Preparing for effective leadership and organization requires a clear understanding of roles, meticulous planning, and the ability to identify and successfully recruit ideal task performers for the campaign. The first element in executing the campaign—the focus of this chapter—deploys the leaders you have recruited for each and every leadership position within the campaign structure. It should be noted that there is no "right way" to design your campaign structure. The number of committees, committee functions, and how they all tie together in the execution phase will vary based on what has worked in the past. Although your campaign structure will probably be different than what is presented in this chapter, there is a set of common elements that should be present in *every* campaign.

The campaign structure proposed in this chapter begins with a *steering committee* made up of three community leaders (tri-chairs), the superintendent, and the school board chairperson. Although the superintendent and board chairperson play pivotal roles on the steering committee, it is best to keep a strong community face on the campaign by having staff support but not serve in one of the tri-chair positions. The steering committee's primary responsibility is to oversee execution of the campaign plan and six functional committees (see Figure 10.1). Command control in this model is vested in the steering committee as it oversees the campaign activities of the six working committees. The steering committee also must ensure that the school district's informational strategies are in sync with the citizens' committee's advocacy efforts.

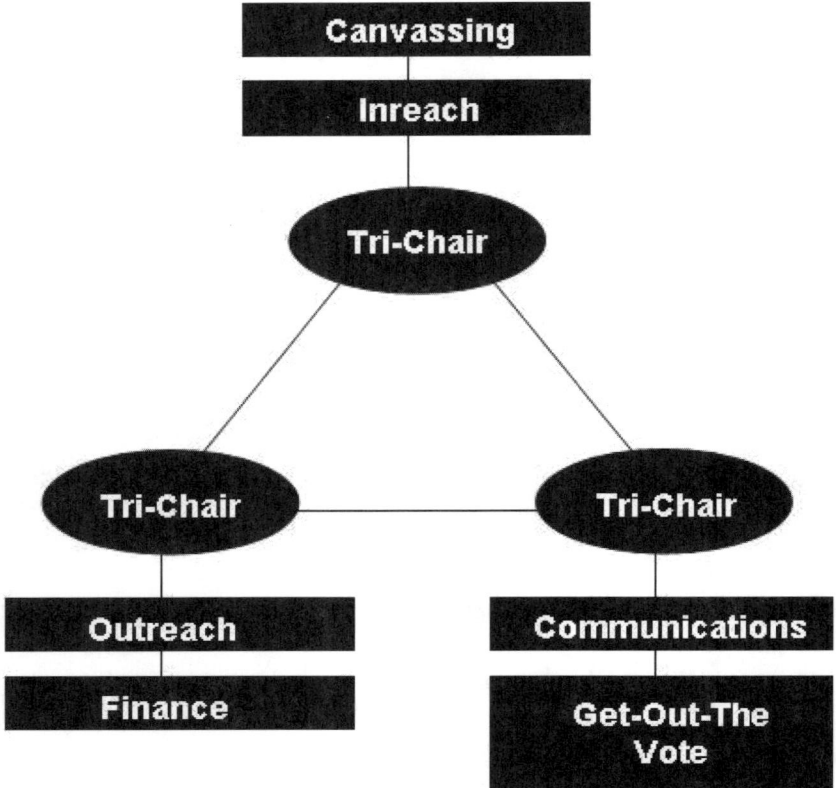

Figure 10.1. Campaign Organization

Although our model depicts tri-chairs, the number of overall campaign leaders should vary depending on the school district's size and demography. For example, a school community with three precincts or wards might best be served with tri-chairs while a district comprising four independent cities might decide to go with quad-chairs. In a school district in which the district boundaries are coterminous with that of one city, the campaign might deploy anywhere from three to six overall leaders depending on what groups within the community need to be represented (e.g., parents, senior citizens, business leaders, or civic groups).

In addition to the steering committee members, six committees round out the core campaign executing the following functions:

- Communication
- Outreach
- Inreach
- Canvassing
- Finance
- Get-out-the-vote

For each of the six committees, we recommend identifying cochairs—again, community leaders rather than staff—to divide the responsibility and workload (thus, making it easier to recruit volunteers to leadership positions) and to broaden the number of individuals involved in the campaign. In addition to the steering committee and cochairs of the six committees, we recommend including a teacher leader and principal. Depending on how many community leaders are selected for the steering committee, most campaigns using this model end up with a steering committee of 5 to 8 individuals and a total of 18 to 20 members on the broader campaign committee.

Our proposed campaign organization structure also lends itself to effectively involving school board members in the campaign. School board members are often unsure how to best engage and be supportive without overstepping their appropriate role or losing the community face of the citizens' campaign. One way to achieve both goals is to ask each of your school board members to serve on one of the six working committees in an exofficio capacity. By doing so, school board members can show interest and provide support while functioning as information conduits between the campaign and the full school board. Additionally, we recommend district staff be assigned to serve as contacts for each of the six committees to the extent that committee cochairs have questions or need information.

The remainder of this chapter highlights the key responsibilities and tasks of the steering committee and six working committees.

STEERING COMMITTEE

As stated previously, the campaign's steering committee represents command control. This leadership role begins broadly at a strategic level as the superintendent works closely with citizen leaders to present and discuss election research, survey results, community norms and history, and unique circumstances supporting the strategic plan for the school finance election. The steering committee also plays a pivotal role in luring ideal task performers to leadership positions on the six working committees. Once the campaign leadership roles are fully staffed, the tri-chairs work closely with the superintendent to ensure that vital campaign activities are done well, on time, and in coordination with the school district's information campaign.

KEY STEERING COMMITTEE RESPONSIBILITIES

The steering committee (i.e., tri-chairs, superintendent, and school board chairperson) functions as central command for executing the campaign. The key responsibilities of the steering committee are

- gaining influential support.
- identifying a target number of identified "yes" voters and concentric voter targets.
- identifying an overall campaign theme, subordinate themes, and target audiences.
- determining a budget to support the campaign plan.
- recruiting volunteers for campaign leadership positions.
- implementing a campaign plan and overseeing activities of volunteers and six working committees.
- coordinating campaign activities with school district initiatives.

A common problem for both the steering committee and school district is to manage expectations of the school board, internal staff, and volunteers in the face of the campaign's continually changing landscape. Suppose, for example, the school district's ballot proposal seeks to build a new middle school, but with five weeks left until election day there is a letter to the editor in the local newspaper suggesting the district build a new high school instead. Later that week similar comments are aired at a public meeting. What to do?

The answer, of course, is the one thing no superintendent or campaign leader wants to hear—it depends! What we *can* provide in the way of guidance, however, is a set of questions and a general recommendation. When faced with this unwanted distraction, the steering committee should ask the following:

- How long is it until election day? (Assuming the high school issue is a ripple and not a tidal wave, the closer it is until election day, the easier it is to ignore the issue.)
- What kind of margins was the district working with at the start of the campaign based on the survey results (i.e., initial support versus opposition)?
- How credible is/are the individual(s) raising this issue?
- How rational or compelling is the argument for a high school rather than a middle school?
- What did the survey say about how most voters get their information about the school district (i.e., how widely read is the newspaper in which the Letter to the Editor appeared)?
- How has the canvassing been going in terms of identifying support? Is this issue coming up during door-to-door or phone canvassing?

The answers to these questions will help the steering committee and district understand what, if anything, needs to be done to counter what could be a troublesome turn of events. If the steering committee concludes a response is necessary, the ideal task performer strategy should be used to identify *who* should respond. This is also the time to dust off the 80/20 block-and-parry strategy. In other words, when your rebuttal hits the street it should respond only briefly to the high school argument, saving the heavy ammunition to emphasize and repeat the campaign's core messages for a new middle school delivered in clear, concise, and compelling language.

As for a general recommendation, our experience suggests that if a steering committee looks back after the fact and concludes the high school issue was mishandled, it is more likely the campaign overreacted and lost focus as opposed to not doing enough. It is human nature to be concerned about and feel a need to react to criticism and arguments not supporting the ballot question. It is vitally important, however, to resist being pulled unnecessarily off course and distracted from the mission. Although it is certainly prudent to respond aggressively in some situations, the campaign usually will be better served by sticking to the message and redoubling efforts to communicate core and subordinate messages to the right voters. The steering committee plays a critical role in making that strategic call and keeping campaign workers focused on the plan.

The organizational structure depicted in this chapter incorporates six teams within the citizens' campaign committee. Key responsibilities and activities of these six groups are summarized below.

COMMUNICATIONS

The communications committee's responsibility, preferably with the help and advice of a public relations professional, is to translate the school district's information about the ballot proposal into a strong and persuasive advocacy campaign. *Translate* is used in this context to emphasize the importance of common messages—delivered in different styles and different media—coming from both the school district and citizens' committee. Achieving this requires close working relationships and common planning between key district staff and volunteers.

> **KEY COMMUNICATIONS COMMITTEE RESPONSIBILITIES**
>
> Once the communications plan is ready, the committee supports the election effort by
>
> - developing communications in alignment with core and subordinate themes and directed to target audiences.
> - developing brochures, press releases, letters, scripts, postcards, and a website presence as needed consistent with the campaign plan and schedule.
> - preparing and recruiting signers for letters to the editor consistent with campaign themes and the schedule of campaign activities.
> - mailing "yes" and "undecided" letters throughout canvassing.

One of the most common mistakes we encounter—often with unfortunate consequences—is turning volunteers loose without professional guidance or the prerequisite planning in place. It is absolutely critical that the research and planning phases be completed at the highest level *before* the communications committee's collective pen hits the paper in terms of producing pieces supporting the campaign. To do this foundational step well requires both expertise and time.

OUTREACH

As the name implies, the outreach committee focuses on key individuals and groups outside the school district's walls that will have a direct or indirect impact on the election's outcome. Although the focus is often on organized groups such as service clubs or business organizations, it is equally important to analyze the community's power structure to identify those individuals who need a courtesy call from someone from the campaign or school district. One way to generate such a list is to ask knowledgeable respondents to nominate at least five people in the community they believe will have the greatest impact on public opinion. After purging duplicates, the campaign will be left with a list of VIPs who need to be courted. We recommend that orchestrating these contacts be equally strategic through the use of ideal task performer and triangulation techniques from the campaign's toolkit. The effectiveness of these VIP encounters can be very different depending on who makes the contact and can often be more fruitful when two individuals (rather than one) interact with your targeted community opinion leaders.

KEY OUTREACH COMMITTEE RESPONSIBILITIES

The outreach committee focuses on efforts to connect with the community by

- identifying community influentials (individuals and groups).
- setting up meetings and presentations with individuals and groups within the community with the intent of gaining support and minimizing opposition.
- coordinating absentee voting for recent graduates.
- planning and conducting coffee parties or other events focused on small group interactions.
- coordinating voter registration and absentee ballot voting with parents using integrated databases and mapping.

In addition to working with individuals and groups within the community, the outreach committee is responsible for coordinating voter registration and absentee ballot voting with parents of school-age students and recent high school graduates (i.e., typically the last four graduation classes). With regard to voter registration efforts aimed at parents, demographic mapping techniques (presented in Chapter 4) can be very helpful. Plotting parent households, registered voters, and voting history on your most recent election can provide the visual road map needed for targeted, door-to-door registration efforts in parts of the school district. The absentee ballot effort directed at recent graduates will be most effective if the campaign involves current high school students.

The outreach committee's third responsibility is to plan appropriate and effective outreach activities designed to achieve small face-to-face group interactions. These initiatives are best symbolized by the coffee party paradigm. For many voters, it will be a one-on-one conversation or small group encounter that will ultimately make the difference. The goal should focus on creating dozens if not hundreds of face-to-face opportunities for the campaign to share its core message in a more personal and intimate forum. How this is done is left to the creativity of the committee based on the community's unique characteristics. A recent successful election in a Minnesota suburban district was buoyed by more than 100 coffee parties. Another campaign committee hosted numerous wine-and-cheese get-togethers. Speaking of captive audiences, a third school campaign delivered its message aboard a flotilla of pontoons on an area lake!

INREACH

The inreach committee contributes to the campaign effort by focusing efforts inside the walls of the district with its employees. First and foremost, the committee is soliciting the support from employees. Building and maintaining such support throughout the campaign should never be taken for granted. Factors ranging from contract talks to employee grievances to where financial resources are targeted to go can and do impact attitudes among individuals and groups of employees. A common "war story" from the battles of unsuccessful school finance elections features a chapter on the damaging effect of what employees said about the election after church or at the grocery store. While 100% support cannot be mandated nor guaranteed, you can build a foundation with good planning, information, and effective inreach to employees.

KEY INREACH COMMITTEE RESPONSIBILITIES

The inreach committee's role addresses the following important responsibilities and roles:

- Clarifies acceptable and unacceptable campaign activities by employees during the workday
- Meets with employees to provide information and answer questions
- Works with union leaders of various employee groups
- Solicits financial support from employees and unions
- Recruits volunteers in support of campaign committees

Wise campaign leaders will also revisit the school district's survey before finalizing plans related to involvement of key staff members or groups of employees. The optimal roles of the superintendent, principals, and teachers can best be determined when perceptions about these individuals and groups are tested in your local survey. It goes without saying that in some communities the superintendent should be carrying the flag at the front of the parade. In your community, however, the role of the superintendent might best be played out behind closed doors or in a supporting role. The same can be said of teachers or other groups included in the polling results from your local taxpayers. If teachers are universally adored within the community, the campaign needs to craft a visible and prominent role for them in support of the election proposal.

When working inside the walls, use of ideal task performer strategies is equally effective as when stumping for support with the local chamber of commerce or rotary club. For example, a group of school district cooks will likely respond differently if the informational meeting is planned and announced jointly by one of their own leaders working in cooperation with the school district or citizens' campaign committee. If the leadership of the cooks' union is supportive of the election proposal, ask him or her to speak first and then introduce district or campaign committee presenters. How campaign members approach and interact with employees can be just as important as the message and significantly influence the meeting's effectiveness and outcome.

In addition to providing information and soliciting support, it is also important for the school district and staff working on the campaign to clarify for employees what they can and cannot do in support of the election, particularly during the workday. Although these parameters will vary from state to state, one could generalize that in many cases employees assume there are more restrictions on what they can say or do than actually is the case. It is often a political judgment rather than a legal question to determine the optimal level and nature of involvement played by individual staff members and employee groups. Nonetheless, it is critical for employees to understand the "dos and don'ts" early in the campaign, particularly as they relate to prohibitions in your state and the appropriate role for staff interacting with students at school.

CANVASSING

Voter canvassing is the campaign activity we most love to hate, and often the Achilles' heel of unsuccessful elections. When done comprehensively and strategically, canvassing provides the campaign with the essential ingredients for an effective get-out-the-vote effort. Canvassing, in combination with postelection analysis, is also the best barometer as to whether the campaign is behind, on track, or well ahead of expectations. Although the intent of canvassing is commonly understood—to separate the universe of registered voters into "yes," "no," and "undecided"—it is methodology and use of data that separate the winners from the losers. The best approach recognizes the finite resources of time and money, takes full advantage of integrated databases, and concentrates efforts through the use of concentric canvassing targets.

> **KEY CANVASSING COMMITTEE RESPONSIBILITIES**
>
> The canvassing effort focuses on these key activities:
>
> - Conducting phone or door-to-door canvass using concentric target groups identified by the steering committee
> - Identifying "yes," "undecided," and "no" voters
> - Soliciting names for endorsements and lawn signs
> - Providing names and addresses to the communication committee for mailings
> - Providing names, addresses, and phone numbers to the GOTV committee for GOTV efforts

In most communities, the limitations of time, money, and volunteers inevitably limit the scope of canvassing, whether by foot or by phone. This reality should not, however, result in a random abstract approach using the local phone book or unidentified parcels on a demographic map. If your campaign either cannot or chooses not to canvass each and every household, it is incumbent that it use available databases, survey results, count book, and mapping technology to canvass the *right* households in the *optimal* order. Again, finite campaign resources need to be targeted to maximize return in terms of identifying support and eventually getting it to the polls on election day. Canvassing done in this manner—whether it is door-to-door or by telephone—utilizes integrated databases (typically a parent file integrated with registered voter data) through a set of concentric target groups.

Identification of targeted groups within the context of registered voters is nothing new to partisan elections, but has been little used in school district campaigns. Setting concentric targets for canvassing begins by asking three key questions:

- Where is our support? Answer: Look at your survey.
- How many individuals belong to that particular voting bloc? Answer: Look at your count book.
- How likely is it that this bloc of individuals will vote? Answer: Look at your voter history.

Through strategic use of these complementary planning resources, the campaign's steering committee can establish concentric targets similar to the following example:

- Target 1: Registered parents who are also frequent voters
- Target 2: Registered parents who are infrequent voters
- Target 3: Parents who are not registered voters
- Target 4: Alumni parents (youngest child has graduated from public schools)
- Target 5: Parents of preschoolers (oldest child has not yet entered public school)
- Target 6: Voters who have made donations to your public school foundation
- Target 7: Past supporters
- Target 8: Democrats (if your database identifies party and survey results indicate Democrats are more supportive)
- Target 9: Registered voters who always vote in school district elections

While the makeup of the concentric target groups will vary from district to district, the strategy remains the same — start at the core with the largest bloc of supportive voters (based on survey results and count book), and who also have the best voting records (based on postelection analysis). From the inside out — moving through one target group after another — the canvassing process identifies supporters, and in so doing inches ever closer to the target number of "yes" voters needed on election day. Being thoughtful and strategic about whom you talk to and when also benefits the election campaign by avoiding wasting time on the wrong voters. A door-to-door canvass can benefit from the same strategy and obtain similarly positive results using integrated databases and mapping technology. Skillful use of these resources will send door-to-door canvassers to the right homes using the identical concentric targeting approach.

Canvassing on a platform of integrated databases also pays dividends late in the campaign. Let's say it is November 2 and the campaign has one day left before election day and there are 800 voters on the "undecided" list based on canvassing. Assuming the campaign is still 300 votes short of its target in terms of needed "yes" votes, there is a need to dust off and revisit this "undecided" pool of potential voters. With only hours to go before the polls open, how might the citizens' committee approach this challenge? The best approach might be to identify and pull a second set of concentric targets focused only on the 800 "undecided" voters. Target 1 could be "undecided" parents among that group of 800 who have been frequent voters in the past. Once the parent bloc is exhausted, the campaign could turn its attention to alumni parents who are frequent voters. The third target from this group of "undecided" voters might be younger adults with preschool children. Again, the point is that time and human resources are finite commodities—being strategic and setting priorities related to which voters among the 800 "undecided" to interact with can be the difference between winning and losing the election. Use of integrated databases and concentric strategies allows the campaign to produce targeted lists instantaneously and is far more effective than simply working through an alphabetical list.

This general approach also applies after the canvassing is done as the steering committee determines how to use the canvassing data to its best advantage from the conclusion of canvassing through election day. Figure 10.2 shows a chart produced by Todd Rapp of Himle Horner that reflects this parallel strategy by depicting the concentration of

	Supporter	Undecided	Opponent
Very Likely Voter	GOTV	Heavy Persuasion	Neutralize
Somewhat Likely Voter	Persuasion & GOTV	Moderate Persuasion	Ignore
Unlikely Voter	Persuasion	Ignore	Ignore

Used with permission of Todd Rapp, Himle Horner, Inc.

Figure 10.2. Targeting Voters

campaign resources in direct relationship to the disposition and voting records of residents within the school district. As reflected in this graphic, how the citizens' committee engages with different blocs of voters should vary depending on their level of support and the likelihood of individuals and groups to cast ballots.

Based on successful practices in many school district finance elections, we are also able to recommend the following tactical approaches that, in combination, can mean the difference between a successful and a disappointing canvass:

- Use multiple canvassing teams, each working two or three nights, rather than one team of canvassers taking on the entire project. This approach makes it easier to recruit volunteers (e.g., "You only have to work two nights."), avoids burnout for the same reason, and significantly expands the number of individuals involved in the campaign.
- Set your campaign target at 130% of your best-educated guess in terms of the number of "yes" voters you need to deliver to the polls on election day. This strategy provides the campaign with margin and allows for some slippage for misidentified "yes" voters or a less-than-stellar get-out-the-vote effort on election day.
- Discount identified male supporters by 0.25 to reflect three realities about male voters: they are less likely than women to vote in a school election; they are more likely to be Republican than Democrat; and they are less likely to be supportive of a school finance proposal than women (Flanigan & Zingale, 1998). If a two-voter household (one male and one female) were canvassed using this tactic, and two "yes" votes were identified, the household would be counted as 1.75 "yes" votes on the way to the campaign target. Again, this approach provides some margin and, in combination with the 130% tactic, avoids the mistake of overestimating support.
- Conduct phone canvassing at a central location, after volunteers have been trained and with the support of at least one, and preferably two, representatives from the school administration or school board in attendance.

- When phone canvassing, always have two more lines available than volunteer callers. This allows volunteers to hand off more difficult calls to an administrator or school board member without having to wait for that line to clear before continuing the canvassing.
- Plan ahead for handling of data and record keeping before the canvassing process begins. This can range from paper and pencil (not recommended) to managing your own databases to using sophisticated campaign software specifically designed for school elections. Regardless of your approach, you need to record accurately and be able to effectively use the data for communications and get-out-the-vote efforts.

FINANCE

The finance committee's role is fairly straightforward with only one significant recommendation based on best practices across the country. Similar to our earlier emphasis that districts should never start writing a proposal before the research and planning steps are done, finance committees are wise to delay fund-raising until the school board is clear on the ballot question and the steering committee has determined how much money is needed and for what purpose. Raising money is seldom easy, but it is certainly more daunting when those asking for the money do not know for certain what the election is about or how the citizens' committee intends to use requested donations.

KEY FINANCE COMMITTEE RESPONSIBILITIES

The key activities of the finance committee are

- soliciting sufficient donations to finance the campaign activities developed by the steering committee.
- monitoring committee budgets.
- maintaining records of receipts and expenses.
- completing required financial reports during and after the election.

It is the steering committee's responsibility to determine what is needed to win the election (e.g., election consultation, scientific survey, demographic mapping, public relations expertise, or database management) and the funding needed to pay for these resources. The finance committee has its walking orders once the school board has finalized the ballot proposal and the steering committee has approved a campaign budget. Strategies for raising the needed resources will vary from community to community, but one variable is constant: if the committee cannot raise the necessary money to run a winning campaign, it probably cannot win the election.

GET-OUT-THE-VOTE

The activity of the get-out-the-vote (GOTV) committee is short-lived but critical to the success of a school finance election. In a nutshell, it is the committee's responsibility to get every identified "yes" voter to the polls on election day. At a minimum, this requires get-out-the-vote reminder calls on the day of the election, unless prohibited by state law. Successful practice and common sense dictate the reminder calls be *on* election day rather than a day or two before for the same reason that one would set a Palm Pilot alarm on your wedding anniversary if the purpose were to pick up flowers on the way home. Having the alarm ring (get-out-the-vote reminder call) on Monday to remember to pick up flowers (vote) on Tuesday does not have the same sense of urgency. A message of "The polls are open now and we anticipate a very close vote" is more likely to get a voter off the couch and to the polls as opposed to "Don't forget to vote tomorrow."[1]

KEY GOTV COMMITTEE RESPONSIBILITIES

The key activities of the GOTV committee are

- delivering every identified "yes" voter to the ballot box through either absentee voting or participation on election day.
- completing reminder calls, e-mail contacts, and targeted, door-to-door efforts on election day.
- providing transportation to any "yes" voter needing a ride to the polls.
- providing childcare to any "yes" voters needing assistance to vote.

Depending on your state's election laws, GOTV efforts sometimes include poll watching or, in states with same-day registration, election day efforts to get supporters registered to vote. These activities vary greatly due to restrictions in poll-watching tactics and same-day registration at the polls in many states.

Plotting parent and voter history data on demographic maps also provides resources that can be used by the GOTV committee either on election day (if not prohibited by law) or in the days leading up to election day. Although most campaign committees use the telephone for get-out-the-vote efforts, demographic maps can help campaigners pinpoint specific areas, streets, or neighborhoods that warrant a targeted door-to-door effort to supplement reminder calls. Demographic mapping, for example, might identify 10 adjacent homes on a particular street, all of which contain public school students, but with parents who were either unregistered or had very infrequent voting habits. The mapping provides the needed information to surgically deploy a team of volunteers to a specific grouping of homes to improve get-out-the-vote results. In our experience, we have seen school election campaigns pull anywhere from 33% to 95% of its supporters to the polls depending on the effectiveness of the campaign and the execution by the GOTV committee.

If we were to summarize this chapter in just two words, it would be "campaigning matters!" It is incumbent upon the superintendent and campaign leadership to first understand and avail themselves of both research and best practice. Once the campaign plan is developed, it is vital that it be executed in world-class fashion—coordinated between the school district and citizen's campaign committee—based not only on research and successful practice, but also on the unique culture of your school community. The margins between winning and losing are just too slim to do anything less.

NOTE

1. In campaigns that combine a polling place location call on Sunday night and a GOTV call on election day, volunteers and campaign leaders are always astonished at the number of people who forgot about the election on election day despite a call two nights earlier.

A Final Thought

In December 1994, the Mahtomedi Public Schools, of which I (Don Lifto) was superintendent at the time, culminated a successful school finance election campaign with three winning ballot questions—one for school construction and two for additional operating money. The following letter to staff appeared shortly thereafter. My coauthor and I decided to share it with you for two reasons. First, similar to Paul Houston's comments in the foreword, the letter conveys the importance of these elections in the lives of children, staff, parents, and the viability of our public schools. Second, although written nearly 10 years before publication of this book, the letter reinforces some of the key messages we have tried to emphasize in this book—namely the importance of comprehensive planning and the ongoing need to build and maintain community support. As we close with an excerpt from that letter, we hope our book has served to better prepare you and your school district for election day success.

December 13

> I want to express my sincere appreciation to all staff members who helped make our special election a huge success. Dozens of you gave generously of your time, talent, or treasure. It would be a gross understatement to say that it couldn't have been done without you!
>
> Much will be said about this election over the holidays by the media, community, and at family gatherings. Only the eternal optimists among us would have predicted success on all three ballot questions. How did

Mahtomedi succeed when so many other school districts were experiencing unprecedented resistance to less-ambitious proposals?

Obviously, the answer is too complex to explore in this letter and would be better examined in a Ph.D. dissertation. There are a few key points, however, that I would ask staff to think about before we return to the demands of our students and "business as usual."

Although extremely important, I believe that too much emphasis can be placed on strategies and the execution of the campaign to the exclusion of investing long-term in building a foundation for success. Successful elections cannot be launched from a swamp full of alligators (lack of trust or community conflict), nor can they stand against the winds of opposition if the campaign is built on sand. School finance elections will succeed only if built on a solid base and fortified by:

- customer focus (primarily students and parents)
- ongoing public relations and communications
- passionate commitment to personal and organizational mastery
- problem solving and continuous improvement
- meticulous planning and execution

Our election was on December 12, but a more important campaign began on December 13. That campaign will measure whether we were good enough in our many tomorrows to garner community support when the needs of children come knocking again. In the months before the election, I challenged every staff member to provide a level of service so extraordinary that no one would ever expect it. Now that the election is over, it is even more important to maintain this covenant with our students and parents. Those of you who have taken this into your heart and soul are the building blocks of the next celebration.

Don Lifto, Superintendent

Bibliography

Allen, A. L. (1985). Predictors of voting behavior in school financial referenda (doctoral dissertation, University of Missouri, Columbia, 1985). *Dissertation Abstracts International, 47,* 719.

Beckham, J. D. (2001). An examination of the influence of technology inclusion in determining the outcome of school bond issue elections in Oklahoma (doctoral dissertation, University of Oklahoma, 2001). *Dissertation Abstracts International, 62,* 85.

Blount, K. D. (1991). The relationship between school tax election outcomes, selected population characteristics, and selected campaign strategies in Louisiana from 1985–1990 (doctoral dissertation, University of Southern Mississippi, 1991). *Dissertation Abstracts International, 52,* 3180.

Bolman, L. G., & Deal, T. E. (1991). *Reframing organization: Artistry, choice, and leadership.* San Francisco, CA: Jossey-Bass.

Brummer, K. C. (1999). School bond elections in Iowa: An analysis of factors, strategies, and policies that influence outcomes (doctoral dissertation, Drake University, 1999). *Dissertation Abstracts International, 61,* 2538.

Chandler, J. A. (1989). A comparison of the predictability rates of the Lutz dissatisfaction and school bond election models of local school district politics in selected Oklahoma school districts, 1971–1989 (doctoral dissertation, University of Tulsa, 1989). *Dissertation Abstracts International, 52,* 30.

Corrick, C. C. (1995). Voter perceptions, information, and demographic characteristics as critical factors in successful and unsuccessful bond referenda in selected Kansas school districts: 1988–1990 (doctoral dissertation, Kansas State University, 1995). *Dissertation Abstracts International, 56,* 2054.

Dalton, R. A. (1995). Local general obligation bonds: Factors which have influenced the outcome of school district elections (doctoral dissertation, University of Southern California, 1995). *Dissertation Abstracts International, 57,* 44.

Day, D. V. (1996). Influences on a community college bond election: A case study (doctoral dissertation, University of Kansas, 1996). *Dissertation Abstracts International, 57,* 2336.

Dunbar, D. W. (1991). A comparison of mail ballot elections and polling place elections for school bond issues in Kansas (elections) (doctoral dissertation, Oklahoma State University, 1991). *Dissertation Abstracts International, 52,* 3180.

Etheredge, F. D. (1989). *School boards and the ballot box.* Alexander, VA: National School Boards Association.

Flanigan, W. H., & Zingale, N. H. (1998). *Political behavior and the American electorate* (9th ed.). Washington, DC: CQ Press.

Franklin, G. A. (1997). School finance campaigns: Strategies and other factors related to success (voters) (doctoral dissertation, University of Southern California, 1997). *Dissertation Abstracts International, 58,* 1595.

Galton, L. L. (1996). Understanding the reasons for and impact of one small Massachusetts community's lack of fiscal support for its local school system, 1990–1993 (doctoral dissertation, Harvard University, 1996). *Dissertation Abstracts International, 57,* 944.

Henderson, J. F., Jr. (1986). Revenue election campaign strategies used in Colorado school districts which conducted successful and unsuccessful elections for 1981–1985 (doctoral dissertation, University of Colorado, Boulder, 1986). *Dissertation Abstracts International, 47,* 1951.

Henderson, T. C. (1997). Factors associated with a highly successful, a minimally successful, and an unsuccessful school district bond election (doctoral dissertation, Mississippi State University, 1997). *Dissertation Abstracts International, 58,* 2542.

Hinson, J. L. (2001). A study of the relationship between the outcome of school district bond issue elections and selected variables (doctoral dissertation, Saint Louis University, 2001). *Dissertation Abstracts International, 62,* 1652.

Hockersmith, D. C. (2001). Strategies used by school district superintendents, chief business officials, and school board members to achieve acquisition of a general obligation bond (doctoral dissertation, University of La Verne, 2001). *Dissertation Abstracts International, 61,* 4627.

Kimbrough, R. B., & Nunnery, M. Y. (1971). *Politics, power, polls, and school elections.* Berkeley, CA: McCutchan.

Lake, C. C., & Callbeck Harper, P. (1987) *Public opinion polling: A handbook for public interest and citizen advocacy groups.* Washington, DC: Island Press.

Lifto, D. E., & Morris, W. (2000). Drivers of successful bond and operating levies . . . Q4C at the foundation. *School Business Affairs, 66*(10), 15–17.

Lode, M. D. (1999). Factors affecting the outcomes of school bond elections in Iowa (doctoral dissertation, University of South Dakota, 1999). *Dissertation Abstracts International, 60,* 2310.

National School Public Relations Association. (2002). *Raising the bar for school PR: New standards for the school public relations profession.* Rockville, MD: Author.

Phillips, C. T. (1995). An investigation of strategies related to successful and unsuccessful campaigns for passage of school operating issues in Ohio (doctoral dissertation, University of Akron, 1995). *Dissertation Abstracts International, 56,* 1610.

Piele, P., & Hall, J. (1973). *Budgets, bonds, and ballots.* Lexington, MA: Heath.

Pullium, T. N. (1983). A study of selected factors associated with the success and failure of school bond referenda in the state of Georgia during the decade of the 1970s (doctoral dissertation, University of Georgia, 1983). *Dissertation Abstracts International, 44,* 1281.

Sclafani, S. (1985). The determinants of school budget election outcomes in New York State: A forecasting model (doctoral dissertation, Rutgers State University, 1985). *Dissertation Abstracts International, 47,* 83.

Stockton, D. J. (1996). Influences contributing to the successful passage of a school bond referendum in the Conroe Independent School District (Texas, Tax Levy) (doctoral dissertation, Texas A&M University, 1996). *Dissertation Abstracts International, 57,* 2312.

True, N. B. (1996). Factors affecting the passage or defeat of California school districts' parcel tax measures between 1983 and 1994 (doctoral dissertation, University of San Francisco, 1996). *Dissertation Abstracts International, 57,* 1496.

Williamson, S. G. (1997). Factors influencing voter behavior in school bond elections (doctoral dissertation, Texas A&M University, Commerce, 1997). *Dissertation Abstracts International, 58,* 3015.

Index

3 Cs of communication, 74, 81–82
80/20 rule, 74, 80, 109

absentee, 21, 111–12, 120
Active Voters, 30, 32, 33, 39, 45, 46, 47
align. *See* ballot structure

ballot structure, 64–65, 68; alignment, xiii, 5, 20, 50, 59, 63, 68, 71, 101, 110; contingent questions, 67–68; free-standing questions, 67; multiple questions, xiv, 67
benchmark, 5, 46, 52, 54, 56
boosters, 65, 66

campaign, 68–69, 72–74, 81–85, 88, 90; committee structure, 105–7; leadership, xv, 108, 121; organization, 106–7; planning, 3, 84, 93, 101
canvass, 6, 10, 15, 115–16, 118
canvassing committee, 115–19
CASA (collect, analyze, summarize, archive), xiii
citizens' campaign committee, 100–1, 105, 110, 114

cognitive dissonance, 91–92
committee structure, 110–11
communication committee. *See* committee structure
communications: ongoing, xiv, 69–70, 124; public engagement, 4, 70, 74; targeted, xiv, 16, 69, 75–78
conflict, 7, 89, 91, 124
core message, 72, 73, 81, 112
count book, xiii, 15, 30, 39, 45, 49, 63, 68, 71–72, 75, 115–16
cross-tabulation, 46. *See also* survey

"dear friend" campaign, 38–39, 43
demographic mapping, xiii, 36, 48, 58, 90, 112, 120–21; election maps, 25; practical maps, 25, 38; U.S. Census maps, xiii, 25, 33, 36, 43
demography, xiii, 33, 49, 56–58, 61, 106; asked, 56, 61; file, 57
detractors, 65, 92

endorsements, 6–7, 90, 115

faculty and staff, 99–100, 105
file layout, 11–12

finance committee, 119–20
focus group, 60
framework, 2, 69, 86, 91, 93, 102

get-out-the-vote, 6, 38–39, 112, 114–15, 118; committee, 120–21

ideal task performer, xv, 88, 102–3, 109, 111, 113
inreach committee, 112–13

Less Active Voters. *See* count book

margin of error. *See* sample
message sandwich, 74, 79

National School Public Relations Association (NSPRA), 69–70, 127
New Voters. *See* count book

organized opposition, 7, 65
outreach committee, 111–12
overrepresentation. *See* postelection analysis

parent file, xiii, 115
past supporters, xiii, 14, 116
persuadable voters, 65
poll. *See* survey
polling place, 12, 38, 40, 121, 126
postelection analysis, xiii, 18–23, 25, 46, 48, 71–72, 87, 90, 114, 116
precinct, 12, 16, 25–27, 30, 36, 38–39, 43

quality, relationship to election outcome, 3, 5, 45, 59

RCPE (research, plan, communicate, evaluate), 71
Reframing Organizations, 86; human resource frame, 88; political frame, 89; structural frame, 86; symbolic frame, 92
registered voters, xiii, 4, 9, 14, 27, 30, 45–48, 60, 64, 71, 81, 86, 100, 112, 114–16

sample, xiii, 6, 46–49, 55, 60
school board, 2, 97–98, 100–1, 118–20, 126
split sample questions, 55
steering committee, 105, 107–10, 115–17, 119–20
subordinate message, 72
superintendent, 89, 97, 99, 101, 105, 108, 113
survey, xiii–xiv, 5–6, 38, 45–61, 63, 71, 81, 87, 101–2, 109, 113, 115–16

targeted canvassing, 114–17
targeted flier. *See* communications: targeted
tax tolerance, 51, 58–59, 61, 64
"theater," 93
triangulation, 8, 103, 111

underrepresented. *See* postelection analysis

Very Active Voters, 30, 32, 39, 46, 47
voter file, 14–15, 17–20, 23–25, 27, 30, 36, 46, 57, 86, 92

About the Authors

Don E. Lifto has served as a public school superintendent for 23 years and is currently superintendent at Northeast Metro 916 Intermediate District in White Bear Lake, Minnesota. His Ph.D. dissertation focused on strategic factors, nonstrategic factors, and critical incidents affecting the outcome of school finance elections. He writes, presents, and consults on this topic frequently.

For the past 15 years, **J. Bradford Senden** has helped school districts in many parts of the country plan and execute successful school tax campaigns. He specializes in the survey research and data preparation needed to win a tax election. He writes and presents on these topics frequently.